UNITED STATES        ENGLAND     •     CANADA        AUSTRALIA

***The USA TENNIS COURSE is taught at colleges and universities and used by thousands of players and teaching professionals around the world.***

- 25 Brainpower Tennis Lessons written in plain language

- Each lesson covers one complete part of the game

- Tactics - plays - strokes - psychology of the game

- Causes of errors and solutions

- Easy to remember instructions that can be put into instant use on the tennis court

- The index provides instant access to solutions to over 500 tennis errors

---

*"I have never enjoyed tennis as much as I have since I read this book. It tells you exactly what you need to work on to develop a set of reliable, accurate, and powerful strokes. With Victor Tantalo's advice in the back of my mind, I feel I improve every time I play."*

**- David Layzer, Ph.D.**
**Professor of Astrophysics, Harvard University**

*"Extremely useful in all my programs both on and off the court. For those interested in analyzing and improving their tennis, it helps turn failure into success, and losing into winning!!"*

**- Ron Holmberg, Wimbledon Record Holder**

*"This book has been a valuable aid to all my students in intermediate and advanced tennis classes. Victor's knowledge of the game of tennis put in textbook form is a must for all college tennis instructors!"*

**- Butch Newman, Men & Women's Tennis Coach**
**Trinity University, San Antonio, Texas**

SPAIN          MEXICO          DENMARK          GREECE

IRELAND · NEW ZEALAND · ICELAND · MALAYSIA · INDIA

GERMANY · SWEDEN · JAPAN · LUXEMBOURG · NORWAY · INDONESIA

# USA TENNIS COURSE

**Victor Tantalo**

*Illustrated by*
**Anne Brown Tantalo**

**USA Publishers**
Orlando

## DEDICATION
To my wife, Anne, for her patience, help, and support.
To my daughters, Helaine, Nancy, Deborah, and Lisa.

## TRIBUTE TO MY FIRST COACH
Edward T. Reid, Bowdoin College Tennis Coach, (Ret.) who made my tennis career possible. My thanks to my other coaches, Ron Holmberg — John Nogrady.

## ACKNOWLEDGEMENTS
Special thanks to Saturnino Salas who gave me the final impetus to write this book; to Grace Lindblom for proofreading and loan of equipment; to proofreaders Mary Enders and Molly Pipes; to James Windham, who helped my wife Anne with her art; to Edward Serues, Amherst College Tennis Coach and his wife Helen for their continuous support, and to my New England friends and tournament players who helped me develop my game; Ted Bailey, Warren Bosworth, Norm Ebenstein, Ron Formeister, Gene Garrett, Mev Good, Al Greenwood, Ken Husmer, Harry Kalman, Bob Kiniry, Adam Kubilius, John Manter, Tim Reid, Greg Reid, Gerry Slobin, Charles "Chip" Stone, Vic Stone, Peter Vieira, Art Watson.

## SPECIAL THANKS TO MY ASSISTANT
Charles G. Salas

## COVER DESIGN
Robert J. Hester III

## FINAL EDITING
Jacqueline Hartt, Ph.D.

USA Publishers
500 Gatlin Avenue
Orlando, Florida 32806

Library of Congress Card Number 86-050302
ISBN: 0-936577-01-0

Printed in the United States of America

First Printing ... April 1986
Second Printing ... October 1986
Third Printing ... October 1988
Fourth Printing ... February 1994
Fifth Printing ... April 1996

# Contents

Contents

Contents

# The Average Tennis Player's Dilemma

The goals of the average tennis player are (1) to enjoy the social aspects of the tennis game and (2) to play well enough to accept invitations to play without fear of embarrassment. A few of you may even aspire to compete in local or regional tournaments.

The biggest obstacle to reaching these goals is where and how to get the education required to do it. The number of tennis lessons that it would take to secure a good tennis education from a tennis professional is more than most people can afford.

This leaves the average player (one who plays tennis for an hour or two once, twice, or several times a week) faced with acquiring a tennis education in bits and pieces from various tennis publications, occasional tennis lessons, from other tennis players, observation, trial and error, and perhaps vacationing for a few days at a tennis camp. Getting a sound tennis education in this haphazard way is next to impossible. A good education requires that a structured course of study be followed and completed. Smatterings of education won't do it. Consider how much use you would get out of a course in school if you quit before completion. The answer is not very much. Tennis isn't any different. You must finish a well-rounded course of study if you wish to be a good player.

It's been my ambition to give everyone the opportunity to receive a complete tennis education. The USA Tennis Course is the culmination of over six years of work to fulfill that desire. It is a complete learning system.

This learning system will improve your tennis game immediately. The first 9 lessons will teach you how to play better tennis without making any changes in your strokes. Lessons 10 through 15 will teach you how to select the style of play best suited to your capabilities. Lesson 16 simplifies how to play doubles. Lessons 17 through 24 simplify the strokes and provide the solutions to stroke production problems. Lesson 25 teaches how to practice.

Your game will improve dramatically as you apply what you learn in each lesson. *Follow the course instructions exactly.* Pay special attention to those that direct your thinking, and you'll get the best out of your capabilities.

## How to Use This Tennis Course

Study each lesson until your mind is thoroughly programmed with the information. When you can recognize the *causes* of your mistakes while playing and know how to *correct* them, you'll know that you have become a knowledgeable tennis player.

Whenever you finish playing, look up the solutions to any problems you may have had at the first opportunity.

Review all lessons frequently. Study Lessons 1 and 2 over and over. They are a great insight into the game and yourself.

Never stop using the course. Think of it as a constant reference. Everything you'll ever need to know about tennis is here.

# The Game Simplified

- **Your Tennis Capabilities**
- **The Sameness in the Game**

Let's start with a firm understanding of what it takes to learn to play tennis or to improve your game. The most essential skills required are inherent parts of everyone's physical and mental capabilities. The abilities to run, to aim, to throw, to hit, and to judge speed and distances become built-in parts of your natural heritage at a very early age.

Improving your game is simply a matter of learning the methods that will put your natural skills to their best use when you play. Whether you're young or old, tall or short, fat or thin, graceful or clumsy, wise or not so wise, there is no such thing as being unable to learn the game or being unable to improve it.

## Your Tennis Capabilities

All tennis players have some misgivings about their capabilities at one time or another. These feelings are unwarranted. My teaching experience has taught me that the average tennis player has more inherent capabilities than can ever be developed in the limited time allocated to tennis.

To dispel whatever qualms you may have about cutting an enviable figure on the tennis court, I invite you to take a look at yours truly when a racquet first came to hand. At that time I was half a century old. That's right—I was 50. What special athletic talents did I have? None. I was just another overweight businessman looking for some exercise.

I started by taking a tennis lesson, my first nearly becoming my last. I was so bad, my size thirteen feet suddenly felt like they were both left ones and the racquet felt like an ill-fitting prosthetic device. I left the court filled with frustration and embarrassment. That lesson preyed on my mind the balance of the day. The more I thought about it the more chagrined I became. Suddenly a curious thought occurred to me. I began to wonder what a fifty year old might achieve if he poured himself into the game with the enthusiasm of a teenager. The more I thought about it, the more intriguing it became, until finally the challenge was irresistible.

Five years later, believe it or not, I turned professional, and within several years I was rated one of the busiest teaching professionals in the United States. A number of my pupils traveled hundreds of miles during the course of each week to come to me for tennis lessons. Publicity abounded in newspapers, magazines, radio, and television. I was featured on Eyewitness News, by a national tennis magazine, in the cover story for the Hartford Courant Sunday Magazine, on talk shows, and in other newspapers. And it all began with an unremitting regimen of daily lessons. At first, I was confused and uncertain because there seemed to be so many new and unfamiliar things to learn. Even when I recognized that I was making some progress, I was often filled with a sense of my own inadequacy.

Like the majority of people playing tennis, *I was laboring under the delusion that the requirements to make the various strokes and shots differed completely from one another.* This impression is common and makes improvement appear much more complicated than it really is. The same impression is what generates anxieties and doubts in many players as to whether they have the ability to learn the many parts of the game. What causes this misapprehension, I presently discovered, is the way tennis is generally taught, spoken, or written about. *Players and tennis professionals alike talk and write about each part of the game as if it were a separate entity. No similarities are ever noted.*

My original profession was as a management consultant. It was therefore in the natural order of things for me to begin a detailed analysis of my daily stint. Much to my surprise, I soon made a startling discovery. *I found that to produce any stroke or shot, most of my thoughts and my actions were the same. I was doing the same things over and over again.* Once I grasped the significance and the understanding of how much these similarities *simplified the learning of the game,* my entire outlook underwent an enormous change. From that point onward, improving my game became a relatively simple matter. The balance of this lesson will *simplify the tennis game* by teaching how much of a *sameness* there is in *making any stroke, shot, or play.*

## The Sameness in the Game

### The Shots Simplified

To simplify what is meant by sameness, let's take a look at what a player does when making a forehand shot. A player judges the direction of the oncoming ball, prepares the racquet, estimates the speed and spin of the ball, moves toward the ball, visualizes the hitting area, selects the shot to make, decides where to hit the ball, chooses the stroke to use, times the stroke so that the racquet connects with the ball as it reaches the hitting area, and aims the ball. Which of these 10 steps do *not* apply to the execution of all other shots?

THE ANSWER IS NONE!

You do the same things for every shot!

Hitting Areas Simplified

Swing your racquet as if you were making a forehand stroke and stop it at your *hitting area*. Do the same with your backhand. Move your racquet up and down and study its position in relationship to your body. Note how far in front this is. Your hitting area is a vertical plane from the ground to as high as you can hit a ball. Every volley, overhead, serve, backhand, and forehand should be hit in this area.

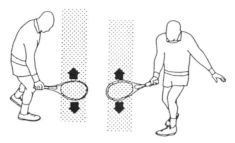

Hit All Forehand and Backhand Shots on the Same Vertical Plane

An illusion that exists among many tennis players is that they are playing the ball more in front of themselves than usual when serving, volleying, or moving in to hit a ball that lands short in their court. That is not true. *When players move into the ball, they take it sooner, but not more in front of themselves.* Good players try to place their body in exactly the same relationship to the ball on every shot before they hit.

Footwork Simplified

When going for a shot, think more of where you want to be in relationship to the ball than of the kind of footwork you use to get there. NOTE THIS: *When you are in hitting position, your body should always bear the same relationship to the ball.* Keep this in mind, and you'll go for your shots with a growing sense of sureness.

The Strokes Simplified

Good strokes are the easiest part of the game to develop. All strokes are basically so similar that I have incorporated the instructions for the forehand and backhand strokes into one lesson. The same is done for the forehand and backhand volley strokes. The similarities between the serve and overhead strokes are noted in their respective lessons.

The stroke lessons, starting at page 143, will revolutionize your thinking about stroke production. You'll be amazed at the small differences in the requirements to make each stroke. Most of the differences are in *changes of the grip and the start of the strokes.*

### Examples

1. The forehand and backhand stroke production techniques are basically the same. The major difference is

that the strokes are made from opposite sides of your body. *The other differences are far less than you now believe.* The lesson on the forehand and backhand strokes *compares the strokes* on pages 145 and 146. *The similarities are clearly illustrated.*

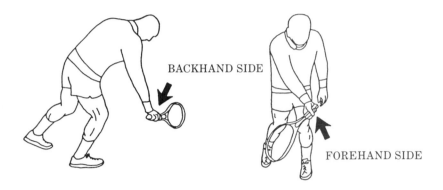

BACKHAND SIDE

FOREHAND SIDE

2. The volley strokes are the same as the high forehand or backhand strokes. The major difference is *you don't take as big a backstroke.*

HIGH BACKHAND STROKE

*Shorter Backswing* on
BACKHAND VOLLEY

ON THE OVERHEAD
Ball *FALLS*
to Hitting Area

*ON THE SERVE*
Ball *TOSSED*
to Hitting Area

**3.** The serve and overhead strokes are the same. The major difference is that on the *serve, you toss the ball in the air to your hitting area* and on the *overhead you wait for the ball to fall to it.*

If you are having trouble developing strokes, it isn't because you lack the talent, it's because you don't fully understand how to do it. The stroke lessons will clear up anything you do not understand.

The Grips Simplified

Grips are a nothing thing to learn. Here are three basic grips that have been used by world-class players for generations. It's just a matter of placing the inside of your index knuckle on the racquet handle in the positions shown in the illustrations.

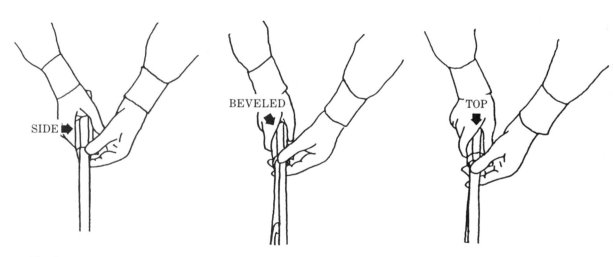

SIDE           BEVELED              TOP

Forehand Grip         Service and Overhead Grip        Backhand Grip

The Plays Simplified

Whenever you learn a play on the forehand side of your court, you can use the same play on your backhand side simply by reversing it, and vice versa.

*Example*

**THE BACKHAND SIDE**                    **THE FOREHAND SIDE**

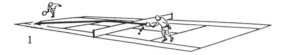

Backhand Approach Shot Down the Line

Forehand Approach Shot Down the Line

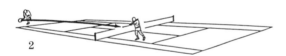

Opponent Returns Shot with a Forehand Down the Line

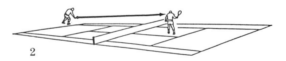

Opponent Returns Shot with a Backhand Down the Line

Cross-Court Backhand Volley for the Point

Cross-Court Forehand Volley for the Point

Tactics Simplified

The tactics that you use to defend your position on one side of your court are the same as those used to protect the other side.

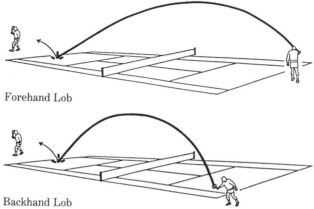

Forehand Lob

Backhand Lob

If you hit effective backhand shots, use the same shots on your forehand.

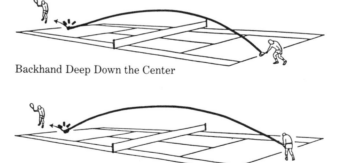

Backhand Deep Down the Center

Forehand Deep Down the Center

---

***Playing tip***  Stay aware of the recurring samenesses in the game while you play or practice, and you will improve your game rapidly.

---

If you hit a forehand volley effectively to one part of the court, use the same shot with your backhand volley to the opposite side of the court.

Forehand Angle Volley

Backhand Angle Volley

If you make a good approach shot with your backhand, you can use the same approach shot with your forehand.

**APPROACH SHOTS DEEP DOWN THE CENTER**

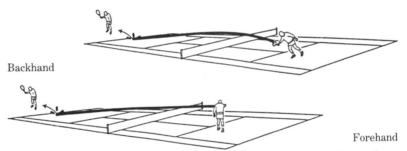

Backhand

Forehand

If you hit effectively to certain places on the right side of the court, reverse it and favor the same places on the left side of the court.

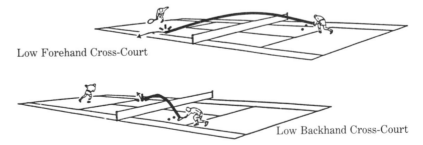

Low Forehand Cross-Court

Low Backhand Cross-Court

Now that you've learned that playing tennis is much simpler than you thought, you should be able to go about your tennis game with a sense of relief, and with confidence.

# Learning Simplified

**• The USA Learning System**

Tennis is described as a difficult game to learn to play. Tennis associations, professionals, and publications all describe tennis in this way. When players fail to learn and drop out of the game, it is always attributed to the difficulties of the game. However, it isn't the game that is difficult; it's the way the game is taught and the way most people go about trying to learn it that makes it difficult.

Nearly everyone tries to learn to play tennis by playing occasionally and perhaps by taking a tennis lesson once a week for a few weeks. Some take lessons even more sporadically.

Whether you are playing or taking a lesson, the time periods are generally thirty, sixty, or ninety minutes. Let's compute how much time this gives you to learn if you're working on six strokes with the time spread evenly between them.

| LESSON TIME PERIOD | 30 MINUTES | 60 MINUTES | 90 MINUTES |
|---|---|---|---|
| FOREHAND | 5 min. | 10 | 15 |
| BACKHAND | 5 min. | 10 | 15 |
| FOREHAND VOLLEY | 5 min. | 10 | 15 |
| BACKHAND VOLLEY | 5 min. | 10 | 15 |
| SERVE | 5 min. | 10 | 15 |
| OVERHEAD | 5 min. | 10 | 15 |
| | 30 min. | 60 | 90 |

In group lessons, the problem of time is magnified. If there are six people in a class, then *the total time that can be devoted to each person in a half-hour lesson is five minutes, in an hour lesson, ten minutes, and in an hour and a half lesson, fifteen.* If this analysis is taken a step further, this example shows the exact amount of time that can be spent with you individually to develop your strokes or to hit tennis balls to you.

| LESSON TIME PERIOD | 30 MINUTES | 60 MINUTES | 90 MINUTES |
|---|---|---|---|
| FOREHAND | 50 seconds | 100 seconds | 150 seconds |
| BACKHAND | 50 seconds | 100 seconds | 150 seconds |
| FOREHAND VOLLEY | 50 seconds | 100 seconds | 150 seconds |
| BACKHAND VOLLEY | 50 seconds | 100 seconds | 150 seconds |
| SERVE | 50 seconds | 100 seconds | 150 seconds |
| OVERHEAD | 50 seconds | 100 seconds | 150 seconds |
| | 300 seconds | 600 seconds | 900 seconds |
| TOTAL TIME FOR EACH PUPIL | 5 MINUTES | 10 MINUTES | 15 MINUTES |

Why wouldn't the game seem difficult? What can be learned in a few minutes? As you can see, *it isn't because the game is difficult or because of your lack of ability; you just don't have much of a chance to learn and your teacher doesn't have much of a chance to teach.*

Whoever "decreed" that tennis lessons should be taken once a week, I don't know, but that's the format generally used. *Learning to play tennis isn't any different from learning in other fields.* If you were told that children should attend school for only one hour a week, you would be aghast at the thought of how long it would take them to learn anything. Yet this is the way that nearly everyone tries to learn to play tennis. With that much time elapsing between lessons or playing, skills "break up" and much is forgotten. The lower your level of play, the more you forget. The result is that each time you go out to play tennis, part of that time must be spent trying to get yourself back to where you were at the end of the previous session before you can make further progress.

This is a waste of time when you are practicing and a waste of money *and* time when you are taking a lesson. If you do not use a good learning system, the road to improving your tennis will seem like an endless trip to nowhere.

When I made my decision to learn to play tennis, I had thirty years of experience in solving the operating and training problems of various businesses. This background gave me the insight to recognize that *the teaching meth-*

*ods in use would preclude any chances I might have of reaching my goals.*

As a result, I never entertained the thought of learning in the prescribed way. Using my experience in training others, *I developed a learning system that made it impossible not to learn.* It ensured the fullest development of my capabilities in the fastest way.

When I turned professional, the foundation of my success was in teaching with this system. Beginners learned to play in a matter of hours, and advanced players made major improvements.

Many were adults from ages thirty to sixty who had literally given up hope of ever becoming tennis players. The learning system never failed. It is now called the *USA LEARNING SYSTEM.*

Its soundness is supported by the type of people who come to me for lessons. Many are among the most successful people in the country. Some run large national and international corporations. Others are bankers, business owners, professors, doctors, lawyers, and other business executives. No one has ever questioned the validity of the learning system, and no one has ever failed to become a tennis player.

## The USA Learning System

I. The Optimum Way to Learn

Acquired tennis skills can be compared with those for swimming, riding a bike, driving a car, etc. *Once learned, you'll never lose the skills*. If you stop playing, you'll get rusty, but you'll never forget. Skills only partially programmed, however, are quickly lost. It's important therefore to *fix skills in your mind* quickly.

Like any other form of education, tennis education should be as continuous as possible. Schedule lessons closely together, preferably on *consecutive* days. The more continuous your lessons, the faster your progress. *Whether you are a beginner, an advanced player, or a tournament player, lessons taken close together, on or off the court, will always produce the best results.*

Always arrange your schedules in this way. Whether you work on your tennis game several times a week or a month, set up your schedule to do it as close together as possible. This will give you a much better chance of solidifying whatever you are working on in your mind. Once it is programmed thoroughly, you'll never lose it. Now that you own this tennis course, you have an ideal learning environment. You can take the lessons as frequently as you like and study the parts of the game you wish to improve before you go out on the court. This is the same way students in other fields learn. First, the courses required are taken and then they go out in the world to see what they can do. Now you can do the same in tennis.

## II. How to Learn

### *Concentration*

Concentrate! Teachers are constantly urging their pupils to concentrate. Rarely are the difficulties involved in concentration explained, and rarely are the pupils provided with a method of doing it. Without this knowledge, acquiring the ability to play tennis will take a longer time.

## THE PROBLEM OF CONCENTRATION

Like all creatures we are in a constant state of alert to our environment. *Our built-in radar or warning system is always at work!* This interferes with our concentration *and makes it impossible to concentrate 100% on anything for more than brief moments.*

## OUTSIDE DISTRACTIONS

No matter how hard we try to concentrate, *our senses dart to every sight, sound, or odor that comes within our range.* After inspecting the distraction, if we conclude that it is of no consequence, our minds dart back to what we were concentrating on. This is done with such lightning speed, we hardly recognize that our concentration was broken.

## INNER DISTRACTIONS

There are inner distractions in addition to those outside. *Stray thoughts* float through our minds without volition and break our concentration. During the time our minds stray, our *learning stops* until our concentration returns to what we were doing. All learning is accomplished in this perpetual *start* and *stop* learning process.

## GOOD ENVIRONMENTS

In a room where there are no distractions, you'll concentrate and learn more quickly than in one, for example, where you would have to answer a telephone frequently or where there is a lot of traffic. The same is true on a tennis court. Your concentration will be better if you can play on a court that is apart from other players.

## BUSY ENVIRONMENTS

In busy environments, your concentration span is sometimes no more than *a blink of an eye* before it is distracted. Can you learn anything in this infinitesimal period of time? The answer is a definite YES! The magic of your mind is awesome. *Even in the blink of an eye, your brain will absorb information.*

## THE LEARNING PROCESS SIMPLIFIED

*Divide what you are trying to learn into small parts.*
Small parts that require one thought are the right size.
They will come closest to matching the shortest period
of time in which you have to learn. Now, no matter how
short your period of concentration, you'll still learn—yes,
even in the blink of an eye. This will simplify the learning process. Furthermore, it will ensure your capacity to
learn.

Using this learning system provides the best opportunity for continuous learning in all environments. You'll
soon discover that small blocks of knowledge quickly grow
into large blocks.

## SLOWLY DOES IT

When you are on the tennis court, do everything as
slowly and thoughtfully as you can. Give yourself every
chance to understand, to feel and to visualize what you
are doing. The more deliberate you are, the sooner what
you are trying to learn will become programmed in your
brain.

Whenever you make *a good stroke or movement,* it
builds your skills; whenever you make a bad one it tears
them down. You are constantly adding to or subtracting
from your skills every time you hit a tennis ball. *Your
brain learns the wrong things you do as easily as it does
the right.* Whatever you do most frequently is what becomes programmed in your brain. There is no way of re-
jecting the things you do wrong until you learn what is
right. It's only then that you are able to correct your mistakes. To improve your tennis game, you must set and reset the correct ways of playing in your mind until they
are completely indoctrinated.

Study, therefore, the parts of the game that you plan to
work on before going out on the court.

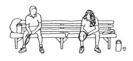

## THE BEST PLAYERS DON'T THINK WHEN THEY PLAY?

There is a general misconception about how much "thinking" players do when they are playing. This is caused by two statements that frequently appear in tennis articles under the bylines of famous professionals and coaches. (1) "The best players don't think when they play." (2) "It's best not to think too much when you play." *These statements are incorrect.*

*If you do not think, your body cannot perform.* Here's an example that clearly illustrates it: *If you wish to turn this page, only the thought of turning it will enable you to do it. Without that thought you will stay right here on page 21 forever. Thoughts are the only tools that enable you to function.*

What is correct is that you do many things *seemingly* without thought. This is due to two reasons: (1) You become so skilled from doing the same things over and over again each day that you are hardly conscious of thinking at all. (2) You are more aware of making a physical movement than of the thinking that allows you to make it.

***Example*** Think of the number of things that you do routinely when you awaken each day. Beginning with getting out of bed, much of this daily routine is done seemingly without thought, yet if you did not think of doing each thing in your routine, you would be incapable of doing any of them.

When you play tennis, you'll make the same shots, the same strokes, the same movements over and over again. As the knowledge of how to make them becomes more and more programmed, you'll begin to make them *seemingly without thought. Never make the mistake, however, of believing that you can perform without thinking!*

During a tennis match the ball acts like a key on a computer and signals your brain for a reaction. In literally *the blink of an eye, your brain scans the programs you've acquired and triggers the best response that it is within your power to make.*

III. Learn One Part at a Time

Your brain can handle many thoughts with incredible speed, but only *one at a time*. The speed with which thoughts come one after the other creates the *illusion* that you can think of many things at once. You can't. You can handle just one at a time in very rapid succession. You should therefore *only learn one thing at a time*. Any other method will disturb the natural workings of your brain, slow the learning process, and create a feeling of confusion. The way to learn anything well is to proceed systematically, learning one part at a time until each is programmed in your brain. As your brain assimilates each part, it will fit them together into a continuous sequence.

***Example*** How does a child learn to speak? First the child learns words, then phrases, and then sentences. The child's brain then puts everything together and the child begins to speak fluently. Tennis is learned in the same way, one part at a time until the parts fit together. You'll find that, although *this appears to be slow learning, it actually turns out to be speed learning*.

*How to Divide Strokes, Plays, and Footwork into Parts*

***Example*** Forehand Loop Stroke

**1.** The start of the stroke   **2.** The top of the stroke   **3.** The back part of the stroke or drop   **4.** The forward swing   **5.** The end of the stroke

### *Example*   Approach Shot and Volley

**THE BACKHAND SIDE**

1

Backhand Approach Shot Down the Line

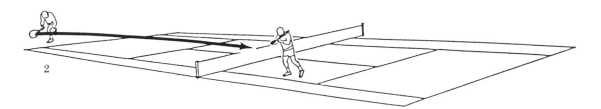

2

Opponent Returns Shot with a Forehand Down the Line

3

Cross-Court Backhand Volley for the Point

***Example*** Footwork

**1.** Stay balanced on the balls of your feet. Bounce lightly while your opponent hits.

**2.** Move toward the ball using small skips or strides. Don't take a large stride unless you are forced to.

**3.** Set up in a hitting position.

**4.** Step in alongside the ball as you hit.

WORK ON ONE PART AT A TIME

Whether you are working on a stroke, play, or movement, work on only one part at a time. *Select the part that is giving you the most trouble* and think only of that part on every shot until you have improved it.

***Example*** If you are working on your forehand stroke and you are not *finishing the stroke*, think only of that part and concentrate on swinging through the ball completely. *Whatever happens to the ball, or other parts of the stroke, is unimportant at this point.* Your job is to learn just the one part that you are trying to improve. When you have learned that part, the learning process is com-

pleted. Now go to the next part that is failing you and repeat the same procedures. Continue improving one part
after another until you have perfected the stroke.

**Example**   When you are working on a shot and having
trouble getting in a good hitting position to the ball, think
only of your footwork until you overcome the problem.
Again, nothing else counts. *Whether you make the shot is
not important.* Your job is to learn how to get into a comfortable hitting position. That's all you are trying to learn.

**Example**   If a play calls for you to go to the net and you
find yourself stopping too far away from it, force yourself
to think of nothing but of getting to the net position as
you try to play again. Again, nothing matters other than
getting to the net position.

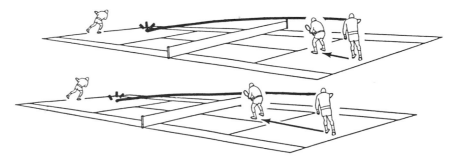

*Apply this system of learning to overcome every problem
in your tennis game.*

IV. How to Develop Your Game

*Practice the Way You Have to Play—Hit Every Ball as if You Were Playing a Point*

Rote drills to improve your game are not for the average player. Career players may be able to afford the time that must go into rote drilling and its inefficiencies. They practice for hours every day. You can't.

You want to improve your tennis. You want to do it rapidly, because the time you can allocate to tennis is limited. This limited time makes it essential not to waste any effort.

The most efficient way to improve your game is to hit every ball as if you were playing a point. Consider the logic of it:

Tennis is a game of split-second decision making, of movement, and tactics that consist of attacking, defending, and rallying the ball. All this has to be done under the pressure of playing a point.

*Doesn't it make sense to practice the way you have to play?* There are many players who look good when they are practicing without pressure, but fall apart at the word "play." The more accustomed you become to hitting tennis shots under pressure, the more rapidly your playing abilities will improve.

During a practice drill you and your partner should play every ball like a point with one exception. *HIT THE BALL BACK TO ONE ANOTHER*. This will ensure more continuity to the drill and give you a chance to practice the follow-up shots that make up the rest of the play.

Hit every ball back to your partner, but hit it as if playing a point. Make whatever shot or play the ball calls for.

**Example** If the ball is short and low, move in and attack. Hit an approach shot to your partner and go to the net to volley or to hit an overhead. If it's a short ball that bounces higher than the net, DESTROY IT! If you are not in a comfortable position to make a shot, defend your position. "Throw it back" (Lob). Your partner should practice in the same way.

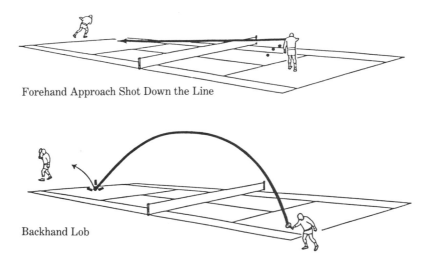

Forehand Approach Shot Down the Line

Backhand Lob

This system of drilling is much tougher than rote drilling. It requires more thinking, more alertness, more movement, and more stamina. It requires starting the drills over and over again because more errors will be made. The benefits, however, make the extra efforts worthwhile.

First, you'll keep getting better at finding the range of the court by practicing shots from all different positions in it. Second, you are continually programming yourself to play under pressure.

### Productivity

Make every moment on the court a productive one. A part of every tennis match is spent picking up stray balls and returning them to your opponent. Don't waste these shots by poking them back in a careless fashion. This is a wonderful opportunity to practice. *Use this time to strengthen your weakest strokes.* Practice returning these balls with a different stroke each month. Aim the ball and try to make a perfect stroke every time.

*How to Practice While Playing*

If you play frequently, change your playing tactics every week. If you play infrequently, change them every month.

### *Examples*

1. Play from the baseline and hit every ball eight to ten feet over the net. Hit every ball away from your opponent.
2. Hit every ball that you can with your forehand. Run around every backhand possible. This will improve your stroke and your footwork.
3. Hit every shot back to your opponent. Don't try to hit any winners. Just try to out-rally your opponent.
4. Play a game where you do nothing but lob every ball beginning with the return of serve.
5. Play every shot to your opponent's backhand including serves and service returns.
6. Play an attacking game. Attack every short ball and go to the net at every opportunity.
7. Let every forehand and backhand shot drop to as low a point as possible before hitting it. This will teach you patience, improve your timing and footwork, and show you how much time you have to get to the ball.

Stick to playing according to your plan whether you are winning or losing. If you have to pay the penalty of losing, PAY IT! You are improving your game in a systematic way. Your time for winning must come. Be patient.

As you continue to study these lessons, you'll be taught to pinpoint the causes of your errors and how to correct them. In your transition as a player, errors are of no consequence. They are just part of the learning process. *Errors are the penalties that must be paid in order to learn to perform correctly.* What is important is whether you were thinking correctly about what you were trying to do. The more thoughtful you are, and the more you analyze and correct what you do, the faster your progress will be.

---
***Playing tip***   Be brave! Experiment! Learn to be versatile.

---

V. The Psychological Side of the Game

*Anxiety, Tentativeness, Tightness, Hurrying, Fear*

These feelings are so intermingled that it is hard to identify where one begins and another ends. One feeds upon the other and the result does more to inhibit your tennis playing capabilities than anything else in the game. Feelings of anxiety about who you are playing, fear of losing, anxiety about your strokes, and fears about how you'll look and play breed tentativeness, tightness, and hurrying.

These enemies are sometimes dormant, sometimes alive, but they are always ready to seize and shake you. They steal your concentration, restrict your physical movements, and generally inhibit your ability to play. EXAMPLE: If fifty or sixty percent of your mind is used up by the preoccupation of these feelings, then obviously you have only forty or fifty percent of your talents left for playing.

From beginners to world-class players, everyone has these feelings. You can never escape them entirely. They will take hold of you whenever you feel uncertain of your ability. To counteract them is not an easy matter. There are things, however, that you can do.

Be Brave. Don't be Afraid to Make Errors!

Be brave-going when you hit the ball. Don't be afraid to miss. Swing through the ball every time. *You learn when you are missing*. Making the shot is the reward for paying the penalty of missing. The willingness to make errors freely will help you become a better player. Whenever you feel tentative, aim and hit the ball as hard as you can. After making a couple of shots, it will build your confidence and you'll find it easier to swing freely through the ball. Be workmanlike about your mistakes. Just analyze the cause and try to correct it on your next effort.

Follow the instructions no matter what happens to the ball. *The more you force yourself to do what you are supposed to do, the more the ball will do what it is supposed to do.* That's the fastest way to improve your game.

## DON'T HANDICAP YOUR CAPABILITIES

Don't place any limitations upon yourself or allow anyone else to do so. No one knows how good a tennis player you can become—not even yourself. *You are all a hundred times better than you think.* Learning is an inexorable force within our natures. *It's impossible not to improve.* Every time you swing at a tennis ball, you are getting better even though you can't measure the improvement.

It's never your lack of natural talent that causes an error. It's just your present level of play. That level will improve as you continue to play and you'll make fewer errors. It's that simple. There are no reasons not to be confident. Keep reminding yourself that you have more inherent playing talents than you'll ever have the time to develop. How much your talents develop depends on how much knowledge you acquire and how much time and effort you can put into it.

## DON'T HURRY

Slow down! Don't just scramble toward the ball without thinking. Players who rush helter-skelter about the court don't accomplish much. All tennis players tend to rush themselves. The problem is most serious among poorer players because they have not yet learned how much time there is to get to a ball. As a result, they let their minds scurry faster than the speed of the ball.

## BE TOO SLOW RATHER THAN TOO QUICK

This will give you a better chance to time the ball correctly. Judge the ball and measure your way to it. See how much time you can take to get set before you hit. *Always try to get comfortable before you hit.* If you need more time to get into position, let the ball drop lower than the position where you would normally hit. The difference between hurrying and taking your time is just a split second, yet it makes you feel like you've got "four days to hit the ball."

Players hurry their swings either because they are over-anxious or because their racquets aren't ready when they get to the ball. If your racquet isn't back when you get to the ball, you have nothing with which to hit. Most of the work you've done in moving into position has been wasted. By the time you get the racquet back, the ball is jamming you and there is no way to make a good stroke.

To give yourself more time to hit, start the racquet back on the way to the ball. Now when you're in hitting position, all that's left to do is aim and hit.

## DON'T BE TIGHT

Tightness is tantamount to partial paralysis. *Strive to be too loose rather than too tight in everything you do on the tennis court.* Grip your racquet too loosely. Swing your arm freely. Keep moving to keep the tightness out of your legs. Exhale deeply to relax the inside of your body.

Exaggerate the looseness of your body. Anything is better than being tight. Don't worry about trying to do everything loosely. When you swing to hit the tennis ball, the pressure of trying to make the shot will automatically tighten you up. By starting more freely than you think you should, you'll have a better chance of not being too tight when you hit.

A tight, concentrated mind and a free body form the ideal combination for playing tennis. Here are some examples of the effects of tightness versus freedom of motion in your legs, hand, and arms, and how to prevent them.

### Leg Tightness

Stand, stiffen your knees, and try to walk. You'll find that tightness has destroyed the use of your legs.

PREVENTION

Take a step and try to tighten your leg as it's moving. Now the tightness no longer ties up your movements. Once your muscles are flowing, you can tighten them without restricting their use.

To prevent tightness in your legs, *keep moving between shots!* Bounce lightly on the balls of your feet or shift your weight from one foot to the other—especially as your opponent hits.

*Arm Tightness*

Grip your racquet tightly and stiffen your arm. Try to make a stroke. You'll see that tightness restrains the use of your arm. It's as if there were a stone wall of tension from your arm down to the ground. The stiffer your arm, the stronger the wall and the more restricted the use of your arm.

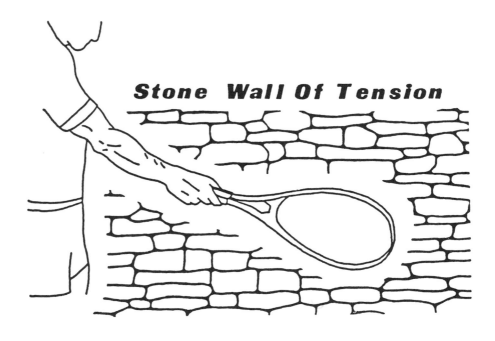

**Stone Wall Of Tension**

## PREVENTION

Hold the racquet gently so that your muscles remain free. Now make a stroke and notice how much more quickly and easily the racquet moves through the air. Keep your arm free as you start to swing; you can tighten the grip as you hit the ball without restricting the stroke.

### Too Much Effort

Too much effort creates tightness everywhere in the body. The ball is only about two ounces and it doesn't take much effort to hit it over the net. It takes timing, rhythm, and an aimpoint, not strength, to hit the ball well.

## TENNIS DROP-OUTS

Everyone gets discouraged with his or her progress at one time or another. When you are, think of what it takes to learn other skills. You wouldn't expect to become a good musician without a lot of study and practice. Becoming a good tennis player isn't any different. Be practical about your progress.

When you have a bad day or a slump, don't get discouraged. It happens to the greatest athletes in the world. Think of a pitcher who pitches a no-hitter one day and a few days later gets knocked out of the box in the second inning. Such ups and downs are a part of every sport. Drop-outs in tennis occur because players expect too much from themselves too soon.

A bad day or slump can occur sometimes when you feel great and everything is right with your world, or you can have a wonderful day playing at times when you feel terrible and you go out on the court wondering how you are going to find the strength to play. Whatever takes place in our body chemistry that causes this to happen is a mystery. It is also subject at times to quick changes. For example, you can play horribly early in the day and a few hours later play sensationally.

The best way to handle these periods is to just accept them all as part of the game and just work through them. You'll come out a better player every time you do it.

# Your Incidence of Error Simplified

- **No One Ever Gets Good Enough to Play the Court the Way It's Laid Out**
- **Hit for the Lines and Lose**
- **Margin for Error**

## No One Ever Gets Good Enough to Play the Court the Way It's Laid Out

To keep your tennis shots in the court consistently, a safe margin of error in from the lines must be allowed for. There is no other way of playing good tennis. This is true for you, and it's true for the greatest players in the world.

*Incidence of Error*

Whether you hit fifty, a hundred, or five hundred shots toward "X," most will land around it in a circular pattern. This pattern is your "incidence of error."

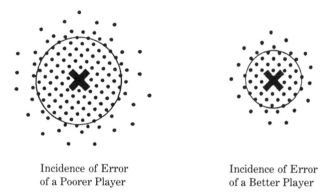

Incidence of Error
of a Poorer Player

Incidence of Error
of a Better Player

## Hit for the Lines and Lose

When shots are aimed at the sideline or baseline, about half will land out because half of the incidence of error is outside the court.

When shots are aimed at the corner, about three-quarters will land out, because three-quarters of the incidence of error lies outside the court. This holds true whether you hit them or the greatest player in the world hits them.

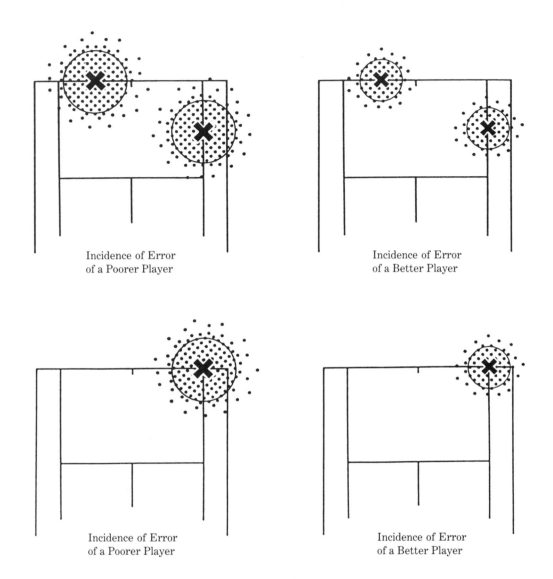

Incidence of Error
of a Poorer Player

Incidence of Error
of a Better Player

Incidence of Error
of a Poorer Player

Incidence of Error
of a Better Player

*Playing tip*    There is a compulsion to hit shots directly at the lines of the court because they are always in your line of vision when you play. To counteract it, force yourself to visualize the lines far enough inside the boundaries of the court so that most of your incidence of error lies safely inside the court.

The great players aim far enough inside the lines so that most of their incidence of error lies within the court. You should do the same.

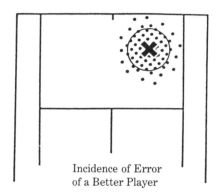

Incidence of Error
of a Better Player

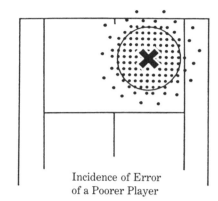

Incidence of Error
of a Poorer Player

## Margin for Error

Visualize a tennis court that you can play safely in. (See the illustration.) Draw imaginary sidelines down through the centers of the service courts, stop them about 6 ft from the baseline, and connect them there with an imaginary baseline. These lines provide a good margin for error. Visualize them before you play and between points.

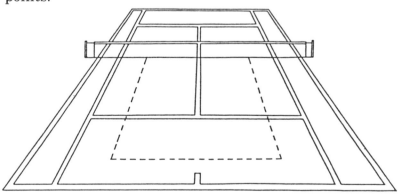

"Court Within a Court"

Using this safe margin for error will turn you into a better player instantaneously. You'll make fewer errors, and keeping the ball in the court more consistently will give you the confidence required to play better.

Two fundamentals that govern the size of the margin for error to allow are: (1) The *harder you hit a ball,* the *bigger the margin for error required to keep it in the court.* (2) *The lower your level of play, the bigger the margin for error* you should allow for all shots. *Be too safe rather than too chancy.*

Just as you should leave a safe margin for error in from the lines, you must also allow a safe margin for error above the net. *When hitting from baseline to baseline, aim 3 to 8 ft (or more) over the net.* The top players do the same. Take note of it the next time you watch them play.

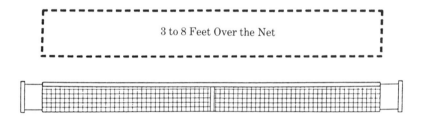

A Safe Margin for Error Over the Net

A lower aimpoint will cause more net errors. Any error is better than a net error. A ball into the net is dead and gone. Any ball over the net may make a point. Players frequently play balls that would have gone out. If you are netting the ball, prevent it by aiming the ball higher. *Too high is better than too low.*

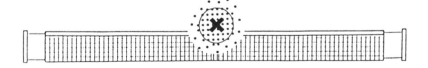

Incidence of Error of Low Shots

There are many instances, however, when you are hitting shots from inside your baseline, that you must hit lower over the net. Every stride taken into the court "reduces" the size of the court. It's essential, therefore, to hit the ball lower over the net to keep your shots in the court.

For example, if you hit the ball from 15 ft inside the baseline, the court is no longer 78 ft long, it is 63 ft long.

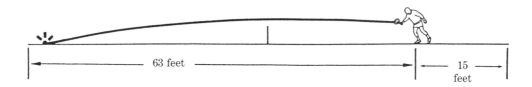

63 feet | 15 feet

The risk of aiming lower is compensated by the opportunity to make the point or to place yourself in an advantageous position to make it. See p. 87, Reason 2.

# How to Keep the Ball in the Court Simplified

• **The Parts of the Ball**

## The Parts of the Ball

Understanding the effects of hitting different parts of the ball will simplify keeping the ball in the court.

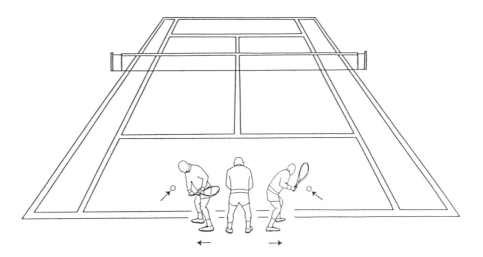

As you move *left,* the left side of the ball becomes the *outside* of the ball.

As you move *right,* the right side of the ball becomes the *outside* of the ball.

Hit the *center* of the ball and the ball travels on a straight line.

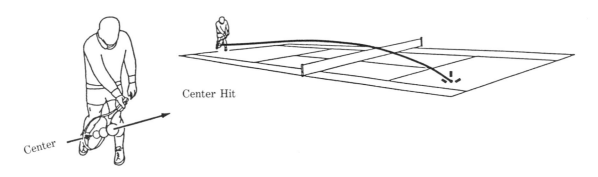

Center Hit

Center

Hit the *outside part* of the ball whenever you're near a sideline. (This will keep the shot from going out the sideline because the trajectory will be into the court.)

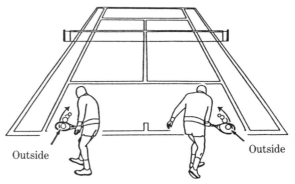

Outside                                    Outside

If you hit the *near or inside part of the ball,* it's apt to slide off the racquet and cause the ball to go wide out the sideline. This error occurs particularly if you are in an open or semiopen position when you hit.

Inside

Ball Hit Out

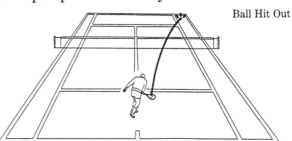

Hit the inside of the ball only *when you have a lot of room in your opponent's court to shoot into:* For average players, 75 or 80% is about right. Now, if the ball slides off the racquet, the large margin for error allowed will keep the shot in the court.

Ball Stays In

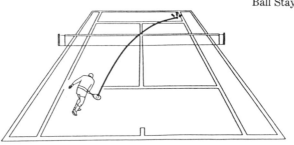

When hitting down the line off a low ball, hit the *lower center* or *lower outside part of the ball*.

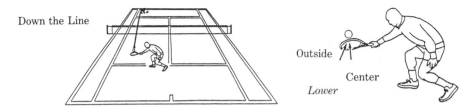

When moving to the sideline to take a short ball bouncing higher than the net, *hit the upper center or upper outside part of the ball*.

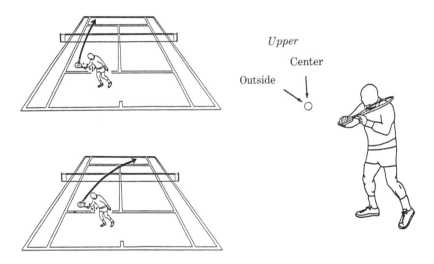

On high volleys, *hit the upper center* or *upper outside part* of the ball.

On low volleys, *hit the lower center* or *lower outside part* of the ball.

KEEP THESE RULES ENGRAVED IN YOUR MIND FOR ALL SHOTS—FOREHANDS, BACKHANDS, VOLLEYS, LOBS, AND OVERHEADS—THE RULES ARE THE SAME FOR ALL OF THEM.

More on hitting specific parts of the ball to make various shots is detailed in other lessons.

# Aiming Simplified

- **Without Aiming There is No Tennis**
- **Finding Aimpoints**

# Without Aiming There is No Tennis

To impress upon you the importance of aiming the tennis ball and the effects of the thought of aiming, let's examine first the control it has over your physical movements.

1. Select an object in the room and point to it. This is aiming.
2. Hold the thought of that object in your mind and your arm.
3. To accentuate the tremendous power of holding an aimpoint, have someone try to pull your arm down while you maintain the thought of the object in your mind. There is no way. Your arm will remain rigidly outstretched as long as you hold the thought.
4. Now stop thinking of the object or aimpoint.
What happens? Your hand loses direction simultaneously and falls to your side.

The same thing happens when you make a tennis stroke. You learned in an earlier lesson that *thoughts are the tools that make us function. Aiming the ball* is the thought that motivates you to make a tennis shot. If you stop thinking of where you are aiming during the shot, simultaneously your stroke loses purpose and collapses. You may be fooled into thinking that you've completed the stroke because the momentum left in your swing may carry the racquet aimlessly past the ball. *When your mind stops thinking, your body stops working.*

## BEWARE OF THE TRAP IN AIMING!

Aiming in tennis is deceptive because there are two parts to it. First you must *pick the aimpoint.* Second, you must *hold the aimpoint in your mind throughout the stroke.* Players often pick an aimpoint on the way to the ball and fail to hold it as they hit. They don't recognize that they have only done half the job required to make the shot.

Once you swing at the ball, hold your aimpoint throughout the stroke. Even if you are completely off balance or falling down, holding the aimpoint firmly in your mind will give you a fighting chance to make the shot.

## Finding Aimpoints

Off Balance—Hold Aimpoint

The Target on the Right is Easier to Hit

In both cases you would aim for the center of the target to allow for an incidence of error. However, you would hit the target on the right more often because the bull's eye provides a more *definite* aimpoint than the target on the left. *The more definite the aimpoint, the better the shot.*

Inexperienced tennis players go out on a court with the primary goal of hitting the ball over the net SOME-WHERE. They spray their shots over large areas and make countless errors.

To play good tennis, you must aim the ball to specific places. Aiming to definite places allows you to see how close your shots came to where you wanted to hit. This information enables you to adjust your margin for error as required. If you don't know where you were trying to hit to, how can you make corrections?

*You do not have to learn how to aim.* Aiming is inherent, developed within us by a "zillion" years of evolution. Man has been measuring distances to aimpoints and trying to hit them since the Stone Age. Even infants can aim. Before they are able to speak, they point at things they want. That's aiming.

*Aiming is simply a thought.* To hit the ball to a specific spot on the tennis court, just think of that spot as you hit. If you have a good stroke and good timing, the ball will go to your aimpoint on the first try. If you don't, it will be necessary to try until you get a solid hit. You'll gradually get better at it and even *a small improvement will mean a big improvement in your game.*

While learning to shoot for exact aimpoints, never look at where you're hitting. Force yourself to hold an aimpoint every time you hit a ball. Keep your eyes on the ball and your mind on the aimpoint. Visualize the place in the tennis court you want to hit to. As you hit, think of it and say mentally, "I want to go *THERE*."

Many players aim the ball haphazardly. They blame their errors on strokes, footwork, and other parts of the game when the cause more often than not was probably failing to aim the ball properly. Therefore, when you miss a shot, ask yourself if you held your aimpoint throughout the shot before looking for other causes.

*Finding the range of the court is the most difficult part of the game to learn and takes the longest.* Strokes, timing, and footwork are child's play to learn compared to picking a definite aimpoint, determining the distance to it, then selecting the stroke, the power, and the trajectory to use to hit a ball there.

Each time you aim for a place in the court and miss, your brain computes the error and makes some kind of correction until eventually you find the range and make the shot. This does not mean that you will make the shot on the next try. What it does mean is that you will make it sooner than before, and with practice, more and more frequently.

To become a truly fine player you must go through this range-finding process for hundreds of different shots to various places in the court using all kinds of strokes.

| | |
|---|---|
| *Aiming tip* | Don't think about your racquet, your swing, or your stroke when hitting the ball. *Think only of where you want to hit*. The ball must go there. Remember, only thoughts enable you to perform. |

# How to Eliminate Errors Simplified

- **The Five Errors of Great Consequence**

- **Dealing with Your Errors**

# The Five Errors of Great Consequence

**1.** Missing the ball completely.
**2.** Hitting the ball into the net.
**3.** Hitting the ball out the near sideline.
**4.** Hitting the ball out the far sideline.
**5.** Hitting the ball deep over the baseline.

Nothing is more frustrating than making errors without knowing the causes and how to correct them. Here are the causes of these five errors and their solutions.

*1. Missing the Ball Completely*

**CAUSE**   Taking your eyes off the ball.

a. Players often take their eyes off the ball as it is coming toward them and don't pick it up again until after it bounces in their court.

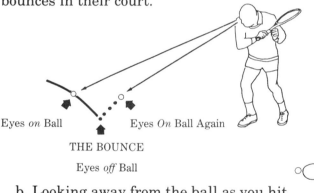

Eyes *on* Ball          Eyes *On* Ball Again

THE BOUNCE

Eyes *off* Ball

b. Looking away from the ball as you hit.

Eyes Focused on the Ball

**CORRECTION**   (a) *The time lost in judging the ball, between the time when you take your eyes off it and the time you pick it up again,* increases the difficulty of judging the ball correctly—especially if you get a bad bounce. Concentrate on focusing on the ball all of its way to your hitting area.

(b) Don't look in the direction that you are hitting the ball. Judge the ball throughout the hit.

*2. Hitting the Ball into the Net*

**CAUSE**   Low balls are hit into the net by not hitting under the ball.

**CORRECTION**   Bend your knees and get down low to the ball.
   Be sure your stroke drops below the ball before hitting it. Concentrate on looking at the under part of the ball.
   Stay down until you have completed the shot.

**CAUSE**   On balls taken higher than the net, hitting into the net is caused by too sharp a downward motion of your stroke when you hit.

WRONG   Downward Motion Too Sharp

**CORRECTION**   Think of where you want to hit the ball as you swing at it. Hold *the aimpoint* in your mind throughout the stroke. That will compel your stroke to *swing out* toward your aimpoint as you hit and come down in a *more gradual* motion.

RIGHT   Downward Motion More Gradual

50

### 3. Hitting the Ball Out the Near Sideline

**CAUSE**   Hitting the inside of the ball.

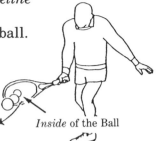

*Inside* of the Ball

*Outside* of the Ball

**CORRECTION**   When moving toward the sideline, hit the *outside* part of the ball and it will keep your shot *inside* the sideline.

---

**Playing tip**   Be careful on balls that come at sharp angles. You see only the *inside* of the ball as you move toward them. *What you see is what you tend to hit.* Hold the thought of hitting the outside of the ball, and it will improve your chances of making the shot.

---

### 4. Hitting the Ball Out the Far Sideline

**CAUSE**   1. Swinging across your body too soon.

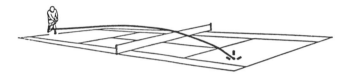

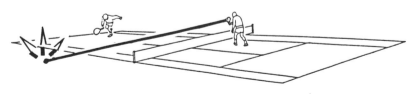

Ball Hit Out

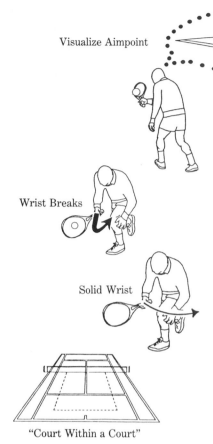

Visualize Aimpoint

Wrist Breaks

Solid Wrist

"Court Within a Court"

**CORRECTION**   Holding the aimpoint will keep your racquet hitting out on the line of the shot longer and prevent it from swinging across your body too soon.

**CAUSE**   2. Flipping your stroke with sudden effort and tightness at the hit.

**CORRECTION**   Keep your swing smooth from beginning to end.

**CAUSE**   3. Not using a safe margin for error.

**CORRECTION**   Visualize your margin for error and hold your aimpoint.

**CAUSE**   4. The trajectory of the ball was too high *for the pace* at which you hit the ball.

**CORRECTION**   Hit the ball lower if you wish to hit with the same power as the shot you missed. Hit it more easily if you hit with the same trajectory.

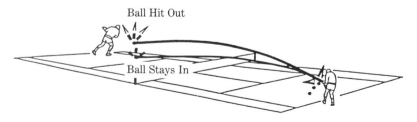

Ball Hit Out

Ball Stays In

*5. Hitting the Ball Out Over the Baseline*

**CAUSE**   Hitting the ball too hard for its trajectory.

**CORRECTION** The harder the ball is hit, *the lower the trajectory* must be.

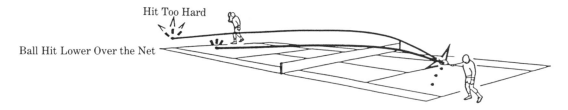

Hit Too Hard

Ball Hit Lower Over the Net

---

*Playing tip* On high volleys and high-bouncing balls, a common fault is failing to prepare the racquet higher than the ball. This means that the racquet will meet the lower part of the ball and propel it in an up trajectory and out of the court. *On high volleys and high-bouncing balls, get your racquet up one foot or more higher than the ball* and hit the *upper* part of the ball. The natural downward motion of your arm will keep it in the court.

---

## Dealing with Your Errors

Remember this about your errors and it will help you psychologically when you feel discouraged. *The best players in the world make the same errors today that they made on the first day they began to play—only not as frequently.* Baseball players strike out, football players fumble the ball, basketball players miss the basket, and tennis players hit the ball into the net.

When you make an error, analyze the cause. Think only of what you must do to correct it when making the next shot. This will reset the correct program in your mind. If the error was caused by a bad stroke, making a good shadow stroke before the next point will help.

When you find yourself making the same error over and over again, force yourself to do something different. *At least, make a new mistake! Show yourself that you're thinking!!!!!!!*

# Timing a Tennis Shot Simplified

- **The Importance of Timing**
- **Two Magic Words**

# WAIT . . . NOW

## The Importance of Timing

Timing is an essential part of our everyday life. Here are two examples:

1. To get on or off an escalator, you judge its speed to *time* your movements.
2. To drive a car, you must judge the traffic and *time* your movements to maneuver the car safely.

In tennis, nothing is more important than timing. Here's what you must do to time a tennis shot:

1. *Time* the speed and spin of the ball.
2. *Time* the ball from where it's hit to your hitting area.
3. *Time* your movements to get into hitting position.
4. *Time* your stroke to hit the ball when it reaches your hitting area.

All in Split Seconds!

## Two Magic Words

Players usually improve their timing by hitting an endless number of balls. This is learning by rote and is inefficient.

*Here's a measuring device* that makes timing a lot easier and improves your timing immediately. It consists of two magic words:

# WAIT . . . NOW

Judge the ball as it moves toward you and say "**Wait**" and when it reaches your hitting area, say "**Now**" and hit the ball.

***Example***   *Timing* a forehand:

1. Visualize your hitting area as the ball travels toward you.
2. Say "**Wait**" while your eyes and brain measure the ball as it comes toward you.
3. When the ball reaches your hitting area, say "**Now!**," aim, and hit.

Saying "**Wait . . . Now!**" won't do anything for you if it's just lip service. You have to really *feel* your eyes and brain *measuring the ball* as it comes toward you. When practicing, say the magic words out loud. Saying them aloud increases their effectiveness because more of your senses are brought into play:

Your voice speaks them, your ears hear them, your brain records them and triggers the hit.

Tennis players at all levels will find this measuring device tremendously useful. Whenever your timing is off, saying "**Wait . . . Now!**" will bring it back quickly. These magic words force you to concentrate on judging the ball. Your anxiety about making the shot will decrease, and you'll feel as if you have a lot more time to hit the ball. *No one believes the difference this measuring device makes—UNTIL THEY TRY IT!*

# WAIT . . . NOW

***Playing tip***   Visualize your hitting area. Remember it. Stay aware of it at all times when you play. Time the ball from where it's hit to your precise hitting area.

# How to Use Yourself Simplified

- **Stay Collected**
- **The Importance of Getting Your Body into the Shot**
- **How Your Shoulder Works**

Generally, the only thoughts we have about our bodies are cosmetic: We look good, we look bad, we're too fat, we're too thin. We use our bodies in wonderful ways with rarely a thought of the magic of it. Now that you are playing tennis, the more you understand how your body works, the better you will be able to play.

## Stay Collected

Collected Body

**DEFINITION** Staying collected means to keep your body balanced and working within the normal range of its movements.

The more you spread yourself out:

• The less collected you are.
• The less capability you have to perform.

Keep your arms in their normal position. *Never stretch out for the ball unless necessary.* The further you move your arms away from your body, the more power you lose.

Try it! Stretch your arm out as far as you can and swing. There isn't much power.

Bring your hand in an inch or two at a time and swing. The closer your hand gets back to its normal position near your body, the more power you have.

Keeping your arms close to your body will also help you move to the ball better. Here's why: If you reach for the ball, your feet *won't move* until you find you can't get to the ball by stretching for it. Your brain then forces you to lunge for it.

Reaching for the Ball

NOTE: Reaching for the ball instead of moving to the ball is caused by an inherent sense of latency that is within all of us. *We will generally make the move that takes the least amount of effort* if we think we can get away with it.

Keep your arms close to your body and stay collected. You are then compelled to move your feet to get into a good hitting position.

1
2
3

Big Stride

Small Stride

SEE THE DIFFERENCE that large steps and small steps have on the control of your movements. Take a large step and try to get back to a collected position, then a mid-sized step, then a normal step. The closer you get back to a collected position, the better use you have of yourself.

Players who stretch or reach for the ball to avoid taking the extra steps needed to get in position to hit are programming themselves incorrectly. Whatever you do most frequently is what you are training yourself to do. Don't be lazy. MOVE!

Whenever a shot forces you to spread out, get back quickly to a collected position. Play from a collected position as much as possible, and you'll be a quicker, stronger, and better player.

### Keep Your Body Quiet

The more skilled you become, the less effort you will use to perform. Your body is the most perfect machine ever created; its mechanisms perfected by a "zillion" years of evolution.

Stay balanced on the balls of your feet and use small steps whenever possible to get to the ball. Swing your arm freely—as if it doesn't belong to your body.

A major problem of unskilled players is that their arms are so tied up to their bodies that their entire bodies gyrate awkwardly when they swing. EXHALING AS YOU SWING WILL HELP YOU TO RESOLVE THIS PROBLEM. Keep your body quiet by avoiding excessive effort and you will have made giant progress toward becoming a skilled player.

### Get Your Body Into the Shot

Players use themselves in wild, awkward ways, trying to get their bodies into the shot. Much of it is caused by a poor hitting position. Don't just run at a ball, *measure your way*. Move easily. It will give you more of a chance to judge the ball and to make the shot correctly:

59

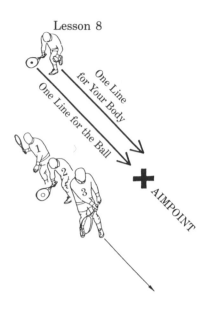

One Line for Your Body

One Line for the Ball

AIMPOINT

**1.** To get your body into the shot, *visualize two lines toward your aimpoint* as you set up to hit:

- *One Line for the Ball*
- *One Line for Your Body*

**2.** When you're lined up, plant your foot, move in alongside the ball, and hit. Holding your aimpoint will pull your body into the shot as you swing through the ball.

*Plant Your Foot*

If your foot is in the air or just landing when you are hitting groundstrokes, you will be caught between *opposing forces.* Your weight will be going *down* while your stroke is coming *up.* Your arm and your body will be working against each other, and you'll make more errors. Get your foot down *before* you hit so that you will have a solid base on which to move into the shot.

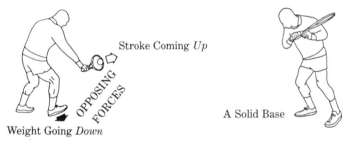

Stroke Coming *Up*

OPPOSING FORCES

Weight Going *Down*

A Solid Base

*Pivot*

Swing Blocked

Whenever you turn sideways to get ready to hit from your forehand side (serve, forehand, forehand volley, overhead), your body is *in front of* the stroke, blocking the forward swing. Unless you pivot your shoulders, your body will remain in the way and block the forward movement of your stroke.

Prove it to yourself. Turn sideways and try to swing your right arm forward without pivoting. You'll find that your body blocks your swing.

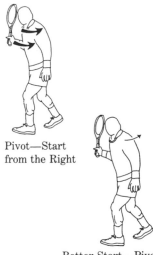

Pivot—Start
from the Right

Better Start—Pivot
with Left Shoulder

The usual method of making a pivot into a shot is to start the pivot with your right hand and shoulder. As you pivot and swing forward, the momentum of your right side pushes your body out of the way. This doesn't always get your body out of the way in time to hit solidly.

A better method is to start the pivot with a *slight turn of your left shoulder*. This opens your body and gets it out of the way quickly. With the resistance of your body eliminated, your swing can be made without obstruction.

On your backhand stroke, being sideways poses less of a problem because your body is *in back of* the stroke and therefore doesn't block the forward swing. The reason for pivoting forward on the backhand is to generate more power into the shot and return your body to a ready position facing the net.

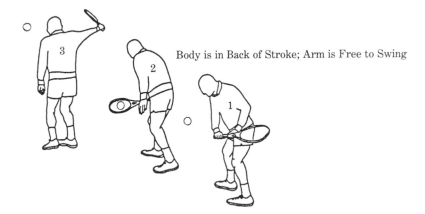

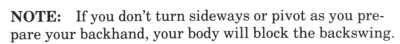

Body is in Back of Stroke; Arm is Free to Swing

Backswing Blocked

**NOTE:**   If you don't turn sideways or pivot as you prepare your backhand, your body will block the backswing.

On all strokes, pivoting and holding a strong aimpoint as you hit will bring your body into the shot. The added weight of your body gives your racquet better hold of the ball.

## The Importance of Getting Your Body into the Shot

If you do not move your weight forward as you hit, you're hitting with only your arm. This limits the power of the shot.

Pivoting and moving into the shot as you hit delivers an entirely different kind of ball from one hit with just the swing of your arm. It has more speed and power, it's more difficult for your opponent to get to, and it's more difficult to return.

Pocket Forms Here

Moving into the ball also produces a more accurate shot by forcing the strings to stretch. This pressure and the elasticity of the strings cause a pocket to form which holds the ball on the racquet longer.

*If you fail to move into the shot, the racquet strings form less of a pocket and won't hold the ball as firmly.* This creates a larger incidence of error and the ball may slide or "poof" off the racquet.

Low Racquet Goes *Up*

High Racquet Goes *Down*

## How Your Shoulder Works

The natural action of your shoulder takes a low racquet *up* and a high racquet *down*. Swing your racquet forward from various positions. If you start your racquet *low, it moves up*. If you start it from a *high* position, *it moves down*.

To make tennis shots, you must hit out at the ball. Pick an aimpoint and *hold it firmly in your mind as you hit and the problem is solved*. The aimpoint will propel your racquet out into the shot as far as it can go. The *up or down motions* of your swing will be decidedly *more gradual*.

---

*Playing tip*   To get the best out of yourself: stay collected, stay balanced, swing bravely, and hold a strong aimpoint.

---

# Court Coverage Simplified

- **How to Cover the Court**
- **Handling Shots on the Run**
- **Getting to the Ball**
- **Your Hitting Position**

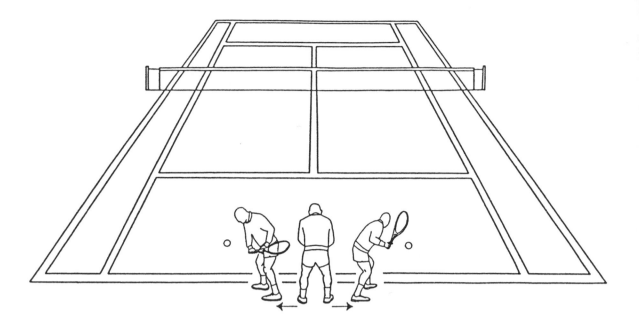

## How to Cover the Court

Next time you're on the court, stand behind the center mark at the baseline, turn sideways, and swing the racquet. Note the court that you've covered just by turning sideways.

Start over, make a skip, turn and swing, and look at the amount of court covered.

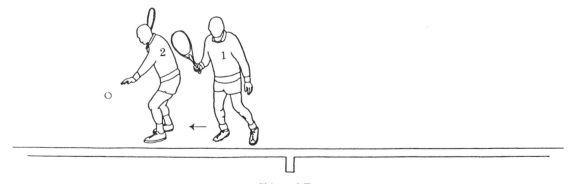

Skip and Turn

Start over, take two skips, turn and swing, and discover that you've covered most of the way to the sideline.

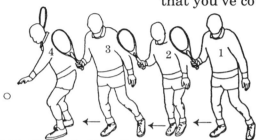

Two Skips and Turn

As you can see, there's no reason to go scurrying around the court for every ball. *Don't run if you can skip; don't skip if you can walk.*

### Skipping and Cross-Over Steps

When you are moving from the center mark toward either sideline, the best way to get to most shots is by skipping (or taking side-steps). To move back to the center mark, however, use cross-over steps. It's faster. Both movements allow you to stay facing your opponent and the ball. The movements are easy to develop and with some practice will become as automatic as walking or running.

Cross-Over Steps

*Poor timing and poor footwork are the primary causes for poor strokes.* If you are too far from the ball, you'll have to stretch for it and it will be hard to make a good stroke. If you're too close, the ball will be jamming you and cramp your stroke. A small improvement in your timing and your footwork will mean a big improvement in your tennis. Never run to a ball without thought. Measure your way. When you are programmed with the best ways to get to various shots, the sight of the ball will trigger the best ways to move.

### Tennis Footwork Begins with Your Eyes

The sooner you see the ball come off your opponent's racquet, the more time you have to get to it. Seeing the ball late keeps you constantly hurrying and scrambling. Concentrate on trying to read the ball early, and you'll begin to move more quickly and easily. Set up a contest with yourself to see how soon you can start for the ball after your opponent hits.

During play, *never look at anything but the tennis ball. Never look at the court. Never look at your opponent.* You'll see as much of them as you need to as they pass your line of vision. Don't be lazy with your eyes. Scrambling because you've read the ball late is more tiring (and more frustrating) than making the effort to see the ball early.

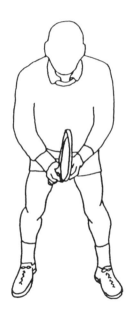

Platform

### Make a Platform

A "platform" means being square to the net on the balls of your feet in a ready position. This places you in a balanced position from which to judge and move to the ball. You should always be on a platform as your opponent hits.

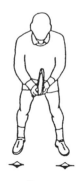

Bounce

### Stay Mobile!

As you wait for your opponent to hit, bounce lightly on the balls of your feet or shift your weight from one foot to the other. It's much easier to go in any direction when your body is already mobile.

Don't get caught flat-footed; it takes too much time to lift your weight and propel it forward to get going. That *first step* to get started takes forever in relationship to the speed of the oncoming ball.

### Push Off?

Tennis players are constantly told to "push off" with their feet as if this were a new movement that had to be learned. It isn't. It's the way you naturally move. *Whether you walk, run, or skip, you always push off from one foot or the other.* Try it. *Take a side-step and note that the inside of the other foot naturally pushes off to propel your body sideways.* The faster you want to go, the harder you push off automatically.

### Small Strides Versus Big Strides

*Your innate ability to measure distances will determine the movements you'll make to get to the ball. The movements are natural and instinctive.* They are governed by the distance of the ball from you. *A long distance will compel you to take big strides. A shorter distance will dictate smaller ones.*

The last few movements you make to get into a good hitting position are the most critical. *Use small steps* to adjust yourself just before you hit. If you make a mistake when you're taking small steps, your body is in good balance and you have a chance to correct it.

When you make a mistake taking a big stride, it's usually impossible to stop your body, get it back into a balanced position, and move again in time to get into a good hitting position. When you get in wrong at the ball, a *SMALL* STRIDE IS A SMALL MISTAKE, A *BIG STRIDE* IS A BIG MISTAKE.

Big Stride            Small Stride

*Cut Off the Angle!*

Move diagonally to cut off shots hit at an angle to the court. If you run to the side, it's a longer distance to the ball. The shot will draw you wider and wider as the ball travels, and chances are you'll never get to it. Remember this when going for all angled shots: Whether it's a groundstroke or a volley, *cut off the angle!* The *sharper* the angle of the shot, the *straighter* should be your movement to intercept it.

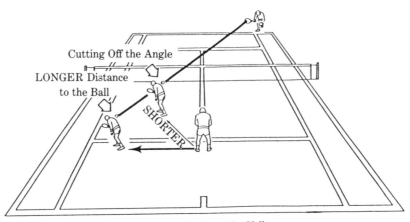

Cut Off the Angle on the Volley

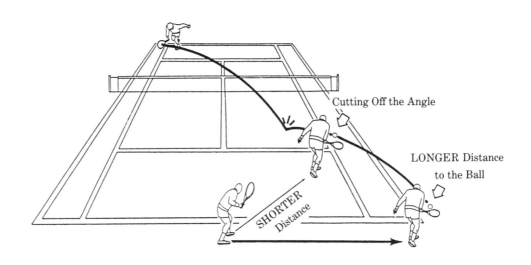

Cut Off the Angle on a Short Ball

# Handling Shots on the Run

### WHEN RUNNING INTO THE COURT

Run Through the Ball as You Hit

Your brain can hold only one thought and give one direction at a time. See p. 22. It cannot stop your body and direct you to hit at the same time. It must have time to complete one thing before it can direct you to do another. When you are running desperately for a shot, there isn't enough time for your brain to process all the thoughts required to stop, set up to hit, move into the ball, aim, and hit.

Forget about stopping when you are pressed for time to get to a shot. Run through the ball as you hit. It's your best chance of making the shot.

### WHEN RUNNING OUT OF THE COURT

When running desperately to get a wide ball that's pulling you out of the sideline, hit the ball on the run and move straight past it after hitting. See p. 84, *Wide Shots.*

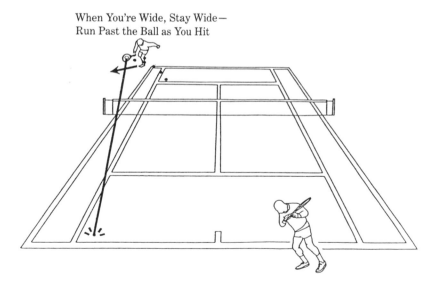

When You're Wide, Stay Wide—
Run Past the Ball as You Hit

## Getting to the Ball

LET THE BALL DROP!

That's the way to gain more time to get to the ball when you need it. When running for a ball, let it drop as low as necessary to give yourself time to get into a good hitting position. The further you let the ball drop, the more time you'll have to get to it.

Letting the Ball Drop

## Your Hitting Position

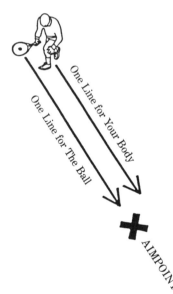

One Line for Your Body

One Line for The Ball

AIMPOINT

Line up alongside the ball. Visualize two lines toward your aimpoint:

• One line for the ball.
• One line for your body.

Step in alongside the ball and hit.
Don't ever stop after you hit. Move to the part of the court necessary to cover the next shot.

| ***Playing tip*** | Stand in a ready position (a platform position). Focus on the ball, stay bouncy, use small skips or steps whenever possible, cut off the angle, let the ball drop as far as necessary to get in a good hitting position, and line up to hit—one line for the ball and one line for your body alongside the ball toward your aimpoint. |
|---|---|

# Playing the Game Simplified

## Are You Ready To Play?

All of the lessons up to this point have been for one single purpose. To send you out to play tennis as a well-informed player. Let's summarize the lessons you've taken to see what has been accomplished and what effects it will have on your ability to play.

1. You learned about the sameness in the game.
2. You acquired a learning system that ensures your capacity to learn at optimum speed.
3. You learned of the need for a margin for error on all shots.
4. You acquired a "fail-safe" system of improving your timing and learned to aim the ball to definite aimpoints.
5. You learned how to use yourself on the tennis court.
6. You learned how to keep the ball in the court and how to correct the FIVE principal errors in the game.
7. You learned how to cover the court.

If you have thoroughly programmed this information, you are ready to play. If you haven't, go back and study until you have.

There is no point in going out to play tennis if you don't know what you're doing. *It isn't tennis if you spend most of your time picking up missed tennis balls. It isn't fun and it isn't exercise.* It's nothing but an exercise in frustration.

You have the means in your hand of becoming an educated tennis player. Take advantage of it. It will enhance your enjoyment of tennis as a player and as a spectator. There's nothing like being knowledgeable.

## What Kind of Game Should You Play?

THE STYLES OF PLAY

1. You can play from the baseline.
2. You can play from the baseline and go to net.
3. You can play a serve and volley game or a combination of 2 and 3.

## HOW TO SELECT YOUR STYLE OF PLAY

Let's talk about your personality, and how it affects the kind of game you should play.

### ARE YOU PATIENT?

If you prefer to work in a quiet, orderly manner and are uncomfortable when forced to attack things in a rush to get them done, choose the baseline style of play. If you choose the baseline game, work on the shots and strokes that pertain to it. Develop your serve, forehand, backhand, lob, and return of serve. You can add the overhead and volley strokes later. Spend most of your time practicing the weapons for baseline play.

### ARE YOU IMPATIENT?

If you have an aggressive nature, then you probably like to attack things and get them done in a hurry. In that case it's unlikely that you would be content trying to play a baseline game. Your natural tendency to get things over and done with quickly would not give you the patience required to work the point long enough to win.

It makes more sense for you to do what is natural and learn to play aggressively. Learn how to go in to the net at every opportunity and how to serve and volley. Place a special emphasis on developing a big serve, a strong volley, a big overhead, and a strong service return.

It takes longer to become a good net player than a good baseline player because you have to do so much more with the ball. There is more to learn, and it's more difficult to learn it. Playing an attacking game makes timing harder. Finding the range of the court from all the different places that you must make shots from takes a lot of time and experience.

Select the style of play that best suits your personality. EGO—our *friend* when it impels us to work to improve our tennis capabilities. Our *enemy* when it induces us to do foolish things.

# A "Don't" Way to Better Tennis

Here's a great "DON'T" program that will improve your tennis game more promptly than any other method. *All it requires is restraint.* Don't be fooled by the seeming simplicity of it. It's easy to read and it's easy to understand. However, it takes a tremendous amount of discipline to use it. Each part of the program that you succeed in making an integral part of your tennis game will mean a big jump forward in your level of play.

1. Don't aim shots outside your margin of error.
2. Don't be tentative.
3. Don't aim for the lines.
4. Don't hit at maximum.
5. Don't stand flat-footed.
6. Don't try to hit aces.
7. Don't try to hit service return winners.
8. Don't hit low shots over the net unless your opponent is moving to the net.
9. Don't hit balls on the rise (as they come up off the ground).
10. Don't be impatient.

| | |
|---|---|
| ***Playing tip*** | Unnecessary errors lose more matches than great shots win. |

*Warming Up*

Warm up with your opponent for at least 15 minutes before you start to play. This will give you the opportunity to limber up, groove your strokes, set your timing, and prepare you to play. Starting to play without a good warm-up is a grave mistake. Without it, you are more prone to injuries and you can't move well. Everyone, young or old, needs time to limber up. This is especially true if you haven't played for several days or more.

## Timing, Aiming, Movement

The ability to time, aim, and move to the ball are the skills most vital to playing good tennis. All other parts of the game pale before them. *Timing, aiming, and moving should always remain uppermost in your mind when you play.*

## Why Do You Miss Shots in a Match That You Make in Practice?

During practice, there's no pressure. You're relaxed and 100% of your concentration is on making the shot. When hitting the same shot in a match, your psychology changes. Perhaps 75 or 80% of your concentration is now on winning the point, leaving only 20 to 25% for making the shot. As a result of this pressure, you make a lot of errors.

Train yourself to think of just making each shot. THE SHOTS WIN THE POINTS, THE POINTS WIN THE GAMES, AND THE GAMES WIN THE SETS.

## Tennis Tactics

### Hit from a Blind Position

Hit every ball you can from a closed stance. (Turn your body to the side with your shoulder down the line.) From this stance, you can hit down the line or pivot and hit cross-court. By standing this way, you are in a blind position and your opponent will find it more difficult to read where you will hit because you can hit in either direction.

### Don't Take Unnecessary Chances

When you are moving backwards or are in other uncomfortable positions to hit, don't get chancy. "Throw the

Blind Position

ball back" (lob) and wait for the next shot. By playing this way you're saying in effect to your opponent, "Here, I didn't like that shot. Hit me another."

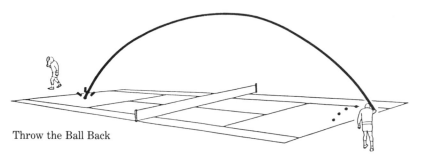

Throw the Ball Back

Trying to make shots that are not in your arsenal is a sure way to lose. Don't give away points by trying to make shots that carry inordinate risks. Don't hit the ball as it's coming up off the ground unless you are in a good hitting position and have a good reason for doing it. Even the best players in the world have trouble hitting the ball on the rise because there's so little time to judge it as it comes off the ground.

Big-risk shots don't pay off most of the time. Make your opponent hit the ball to earn a point.

Taking the Ball on the Rise

## AVOID YOUR WEAKNESSES

If you lack agility, hit shots deep to the center of your opponent's baseline. This limits the ability of your opponent to run you because it limits the angle to the court that shots can be hit. Your opponent cannot shoot for areas outside the ones marked in the example without a big increase in his or her incidence of error.

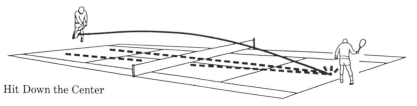

Hit Down the Center

Avoid your weaknesses like the plague. When a ball comes to one of your weaknesses, run around it and handle it from your best side. Program yourself to use your best strokes and your favorite shots when you play.

### Be a Brave-Going Tennis Player

Be brave and be decisive. There are no reasons not to be. A tennis shot can only be hit *down the line* or *cross-court, short* or *deep*. Pick your shot and *hit without hesitation*. Whatever happens to the ball happens. That's the way to improvement. Never be indecisive or tentative when you hit. Be brave-going. If you make an error, make it because you were too brave, never because you were weak. Be brave, but don't be foolhardy. Play within a frame that gives you confidence. Leave a good margin for error above the net and in from the sidelines. When hitting from the baseline, aim 3 to 8 ft or more above the net. Don't hit lower unless your opponent is coming in to the net. Hit under every ball that lands *deep* in your court, no matter how high or low it bounces. Don't try to play beyond your capabilities. It's a sure way to lose.

### Hitting at Maximum

Trying to win by always blasting the ball would be as senseless as baseball players trying to hit home runs on every pitch or basketball players shooting for the basket whenever they got the ball, no matter where they were in the court, or quarterbacks always trying 60 or 70 yard passes for touchdowns. There's no way to win this way.

There's enough pressure in playing without manufacturing more by trying to hit hard all the time. *You're at a cracking point whenever you hit at maximum.* Hit at maximum only when you have a reason, and not just for the sake of hitting balls hard.

The sign of a skilled player is having the capability of doing just what is necessary to win the point. Always play the shot that your position in the court and to the ball calls for. Never more.

*Exploit Your Opponent's Weaknesses*

During a match, remind yourself that you are not out there to make great shots, to look good, or to hit the shots that you enjoy hitting. You're out there to win.

One way to win is to simply try to outlast your opponent in a rally. If your opponent misses every third shot and you are capable of hitting one more ball in the court than your opponent, the match is over.

You win by hurting your opponent in some way. • Move the ball. That hurts everyone. Every step or movement you force your opponent to make increases your chances of drawing an error. • Hit shots your opponent doesn't like. No one likes high, deep balls to his or her backhand. • Hit shots that crowd your opponent. Shots that jam a player's movements are hard to handle. Big opponents especially don't like them because it's so hard for them to get out of the way of the ball and into position to hit. • Low shots are also difficult for big players because it's hard for them to bend down in a low position and stay there while they make the shot. • If your opponent lacks stamina, hit the shots that compel a player to run the most. Cross-courts, drop-shots, and chip-shots are the shots to play. • If your opponent can't hit overheads, lob the ball frequently.

*Changes of Pace*

Hit at various heights and speeds to keep your opponent off-balance and uncomfortable. If you can slice or hit with topspin as well as drive, then mix them up. The more you force your opponent to keep judging different shots, the more it will tire your opponent mentally and the more points you'll win.

At the other end of the spectrum, look for changes of pace from your opponent. Program and reprogram yourself to look for changes of pace. This will give you a mental readiness that will enable you to recognize the changes and handle them more easily. EXAMPLE: If you expect drop-shots, it's a lot easier to get to them.

*The Control of the Court*

WHAT IS DEEP?

Maintain control of the court by hitting the ball deep. The term, "hit the ball deep," is misunderstood. *It's generally believed that it means hitting the ball to your opponent's baseline.* That's only a partial definition and is not always true.

*The true definition is to hit the ball deep to your opponent's position in the court.* If your opponent is at or behind the baseline, then deep means to hit to the baseline.

Deep to Opponent

When your opponent moves into the court, you no longer have to hit near the baseline because now *deep is anything that is at your opponent's feet or beyond.*

If your opponent is near the service line, for example, all you have to do is hit the ball past the service line. There's no point in going for the baseline and taking the added risk of knocking the ball out.

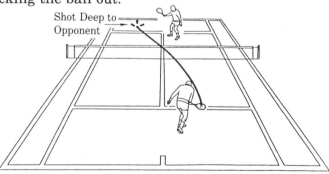

Shot Deep to Opponent

So, hitting deep means HITTING DEEP TO YOUR OPPONENT WHEREVER HE OR SHE MAY BE ON THE COURT.

Aim your shots deep. Deep balls are hard for anyone to handle and tend to produce short returns and errors. When you are in a baseline rally, concentrate on hitting under every ball, and aiming 3 to 8 ft (or more) above the net. This will help you keep the ball deep and maintain control of the court. Playing the ball deep will also give you more time to get back in position to play the next shot.

Focus on the ball and make up your mind that if you're going to make an error, you're going to make it by hitting the ball over the baseline. That's the easiest error to correct.

When you hit the ball over the baseline, you've hit the ball too hard for its trajectory. If you want to hit the next ball at the *same trajectory*, hit it *easier* to keep it in the court. If you want to hit at the *same speed, lower the trajectory*.

Ball Hit Too Hard for Trajectory

Ball Hit at Same Speed,
Hit at Lower Trajectory

Ball Hit at Same Trajectory,
Hit Easier

Whenever you hit short in a rally from the baseline, you lose *control of the court*. Your opponent can attack and has many opportunities to make the point. Your opponent can make the point:

**1.** By taking the ball early and hitting a winner.
**2.** By making an approach shot and coming in to the net.
**3.** By hitting a drop-shot, chip-shot, angle shot, etc.

Always be aware that when you are in a rally from the baseline, you are fencing with your opponent to see who is going to lose the control of the court.

*Taking the Ball Early*

The advantage of moving in to the court and taking the ball early is that the ball gets to your opponent sooner.

This increases your chances of winning a point.

The best way to illustrate how much sooner the ball gets to your opponent's court is to relate it to the length of the court. EXAMPLE: The distance from the baseline to the net is 39 ft. If a ball bounces at the service line and you wait for it at the baseline, the ball travels 18 ft. It's another 18 ft back to the point where it bounced. That's a total of 36 ft the ball travels. That's just 3 ft less than the length of the court from the net to the baseline.

Now suppose that you move 10 ft into the court to take the ball. *Moving in 10 ft saves 10 ft that the ball travels toward you plus 10 ft that your shot travels back.* This is equal to more than half the length of your court!

Each step that you take into the court shortens the distance that the ball travels and reduces the time your opponent has to get ready and hit. Just think of how much less time your opponent has when you are closer to the net.

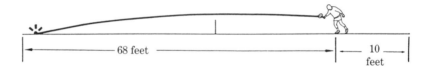

|←———— 68 feet ————→|←— 10 —→|
                              feet

## Cross-Court Shots

Explore the cross-court shots. Hitting cross-court runs your opponent more than hitting a down-the-line shot. Every step or fraction of a step that you force your opponent to move increases his or her incidence of error.

Strategically, there are literally hundreds of possible cross-court shots and angles.

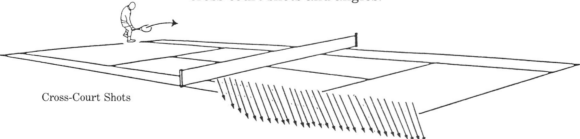

Cross-Court Shots

Down-the-line shots are just straight shots, short or deep.

Down-the-Line

There is also less of a risk factor in hitting shots cross-court because the court is longer diagonally and the shot travels over the lower part of the net. Running your opponents cross-court will tire them more, and tired players make more errors.

*Beware of This Mistake*

Innumerable errors are made by average players who try to make shots down-the-line from an open hitting position.

Big Incidence of Error

If your hitting position is open, *hit the ball cross-court.*

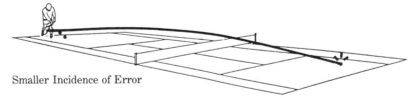

Smaller Incidence of Error

Smaller Incidence of Error

If you hit down-the-line, the incidence for error is much greater. The ball will slide on your racquet at the hit and can easily go out of the court. *Use this shot only when you have a lot of room in your opponent's court to hit into.*

| **Playing tip** | From an *open hitting position,* hit all shots—forehands, backhands, volleys, and overheads—*cross-court* or *down the center.* |
| --- | --- |

*Down-the-Line Shots*

Hit shots down-the-line when you have pulled your opponent out of position and you have a wide-open court to hit to or your opponent is running one way and you can hit behind him.

Pulled Out of Court

Hit Behind Opponent

Hit down-the-line shots to opponents who have weak backhand strokes. Certain approach shots are best made down-the-line if you can get into position for the return shot more quickly.

Approach Shot

*How To Handle High Bouncing Balls, Wide Balls*

## SHORT BALLS BOUNCING HIGHER THAN THE NET

*Take your racquet back and up higher than the ball. Use the heel of your hand to start the swing,* keep the racquet head *up,* pivot, and hit the *upper outside* or *upper center* of the ball. Hold your aimpoint and you will hit out as you swing. The natural action of your shoulder will supply all the downward motion needed to keep the ball in the court.

Prepare Racquet
Higher than Ball

*Keep moving through the ball as you hit.* (Your next position is at the net to cover the return if you failed to make the point.)

Hit this shot hard. *Go for the point.* Don't compromise.

Hit High Shots Hard

> ***Stroke tip*** By far the most common error on this shot is hitting the ball into the net. This is the result of failing to hold your aimpoint and hitting *down* instead of *out*. When you fail to hold a strong aimpoint, the natural downward movement of your arm brings the racquet down too sharply and sends the ball into the net.

## HIGH BOUNCING BALLS NEAR THE BASELINE

Don't hit these shots as you would short, high bouncing balls. Most of your shots will go into the net or be short if you do. Use your regular groundstrokes, *hit under the ball,* and *aim high over the net* in order to get penetration in the court.

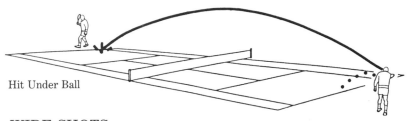

Hit Under Ball

## WIDE SHOTS

Whenever a wide shot forces you to run hard out of the court, there is no way to stop your momentum, hit, and get back in position to cover the next shot. *Therefore this is your last shot of the point, win or lose.* The only thing left to do is go for the point by driving the ball hard down the line as you run out of the court. Go for the shot bravely and you'll pick up some points that you might otherwise lose. If you miss, you haven't lost much because you're out of the point anyway.

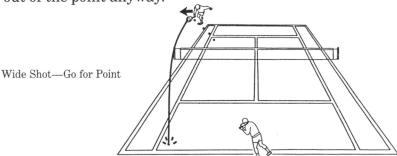

Wide Shot—Go for Point

Hitting a wide shot down the line also gives you a better chance to make the shot than trying to hit cross court because your racquet stays on the ball longer. *If you try to go cross court while reaching wide, your racquet will slide off the ball* because generally you are not far enough behind it to get good hold of it.

See this for yourself: Pick up a racquet, reach wide for an imaginary ball and swing as if you were hitting down the line. Now swing as if you were hitting cross court and compare the way your racquet moves past the hitting area.

WHEN REACHING WIDE

Less Chance of Making the Shot

Better Chance of Making the Shot

Hitting Down-the-Line

Hitting Cross-Court

You'll note that the racquet stays much longer on the line of the shot when hitting down the line than it does when hitting cross court.

Remember this rule on all shots you reach wide for: *When wide, stay wide.*

*Put-Away Shots*

## WHAT IS A PUT-AWAY SHOT?

A put-away shot is any shot you hit that is impossible for your opponent to get to.

## HOW TO HIT A PUT-AWAY SHOT

Take the ball as soon as possible, move through it as aggressively as your skill permits, and hit to a definite aimpoint.

## WHEN CAN YOU HIT A PUT-AWAY SHOT?

- Off any short ball bouncing higher than the net
- Off any ball higher than the net that you can volley
- Off any ball you can take soon enough so that there is no way your opponent can get to the ball
- Off any ball you can hit at a sharp angle
- Off any ball you can hit with an overhead

## WHERE TO HIT PUT-AWAY SHOTS

Where to hit put-away shots depends on your position to the ball and your position in the court.

### *Examples*

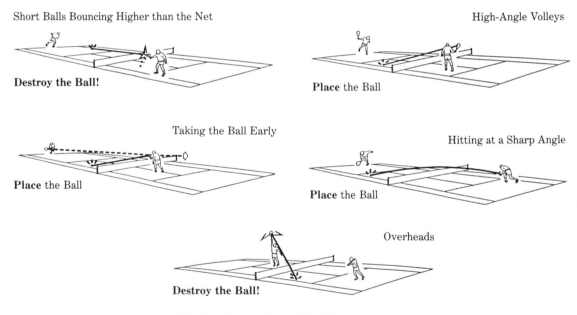

Short Balls Bouncing Higher than the Net

**Destroy the Ball!**

High-Angle Volleys

**Place** the Ball

Taking the Ball Early

**Place** the Ball

Hitting at a Sharp Angle

**Place** the Ball

Overheads

**Destroy the Ball!**

### *Hitting Low Over the Net*

Hit the ball one foot or lower over the net when you move into the court. Here are two reasons:

**1.** The court is shortened by every step you take into it. It is no longer 78 feet long. Therefore, in order to keep the ball in the court, you must aim lower over the net.

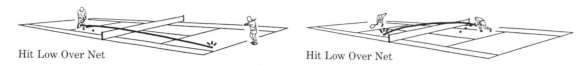

Hit Low Over Net                    Hit Low Over Net

**2.** Hitting lower increases your chances of making the point because the ball gets to or past your opponent sooner. This gives your opponent less time to read, react to, and get to the ball.

**NOTE**   While hitting lower gives your opponent less time to hit, it also gives you less time to get in position for the return.

*Passing Shots*

Go for the passing shot if the opponent stops no closer to the net than the middle of the service court. Aim the ball low past the opponent. It isn't necessary to do more. Don't risk making an error by shooting for the baseline.

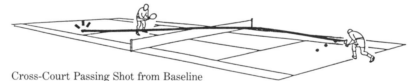

Cross-Court Passing Shot from Baseline

If the opponent is close to the net but has hit short, you can move in and make a passing shot to either side. Don't rush it. You should make the pass most of the time.

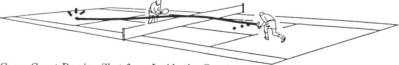

Cross-Court Passing Shot from Inside the Court

If your opponent has hit from near his service court sideline down the line to your baseline corner, then turns to move toward the center of the net, drive the ball back behind him low and hard down the line.

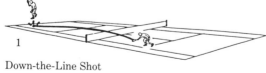

Down-the-Line Shot

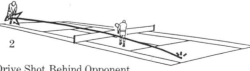

Drive Shot Behind Opponent

In a baseline rally, when your opponent is out of position on one side of the court, go for a passing shot by driving hard to the opposite side.

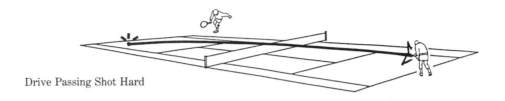

Drive Passing Shot Hard

## Drop Shot

Move into the ball with your racquet prepared higher than the ball. Aim the ball, hit it with a delicate slicing motion and move through it as you hit. Think of hitting the ball at two miles an hour to your aimpoint.

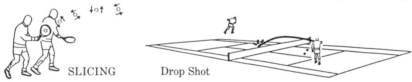

SLICING          Drop Shot

---

***Stroke tip***   There is a tendency to pull back at the hit. *Don't.* Move through the ball authoritatively.

---

## When To Hit Short

If you get a short ball and your opponent is out of position behind the baseline, a chip or a drop shot is a good play.

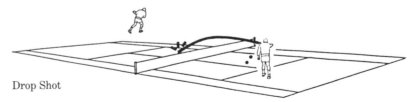

Drop Shot

If your opponent hits a drop shot and the ball lands very close to the net, drop shot or chip in return. If the ball lands deeper in the service court, make a down-the-line approach shot or hit a cross-court winner.

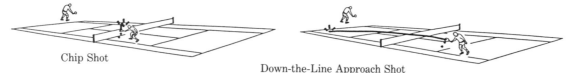

Chip Shot

Down-the-Line Approach Shot

The closer you are to the net when you chip or drop shot, the better. From close to the net, your shot doesn't have far to travel, so your opponent has less time to recognize it and react. Use a drop shot when you feel your opponent doesn't expect one. Surprise is an important element in making winning drops.

You can also hit short if your opponent has been forced way out of the court or back out of position. Then hit short as part of a play.

***Example*** A high, deep shot to the backhand which forces your opponent back and off-balance means that the return will probably be weak and short. Move in and hit short to the opposite side close to the net. If the opponent manages to scramble in and return it, hit a passing shot or lob deep.

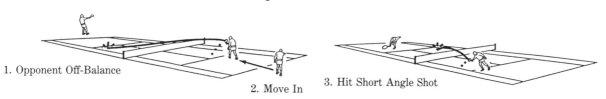

1. Opponent Off-Balance

2. Move In

3. Hit Short Angle Shot

*The Lob*

Everyone should try to become a great lobber. There isn't any shot that can be more useful defensively or offensively.

To become a good lobber, *lob the tennis court. Don't look at your opponent.* If you do, your opponent is apt to be the last thought in your mind and you will involuntarily aim to him and hit short.

To lob, use your regular groundstrokes and hit underneath the ball.

• Slice to hit a backspin lob.
• Hit flat to hit a lob with minimum spin.
• Brush up on the ball to hit a topspin lob.

Be sure to swing through the ball at all costs! Don't ever stop your stroke!

Too many lobs are carelessly swiped at without aimpoints or direction. Lob at a definite height to a definite aimpoint in the court. To aim a lob accurately, lob the ball so that it reaches its peak halfway between you and your aimpoint. Hold your aimpoint and hit through the ball as you would on any other shot but at a slower pace.

Lob when you are moving backwards or aren't in good position to hit. Aiming the lob to your opponent's baseline will give you time to get back in position for the next shot.

When you throw the ball back (lob), what you're saying in effect to your opponent is "Here, I didn't like that shot; hit me another."

If you're lobbing defensively (especially if you're running wide), hit high and deep toward the center mark. All you're doing is trying to give yourself time to get in position for the next shot, and hitting down the center gives you a wide margin of safety on both sides. Sometimes when you lob and are late for the ball, snapping your wrist and hitting a *slice lob* can get you out of a jam and save the point.

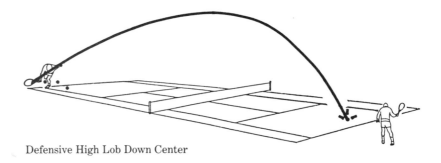

Defensive High Lob Down Center

If your opponent is coming in to net, you may want to try a passing shot with an offensive lob. Hit this lob at a lower trajectory over the opponent's backhand side, but be sure your opponent is moving forward when you do it. Otherwise the opponent will be able to move back and hit an overhead because of the lower trajectory. The *topspin lob* is the best offensive lob because it gets over the head of your opponent quickly, comes down sharply, and runs away after it bounces.

The key to lobbing is to have a mental picture of the court and of the lob you are trying to hit. If you're playing indoors, take a look at the ceiling. Note the height of the lights and any other hanging fixtures. Fix their positions in your mind. Outdoors, be aware of where the sun is and which way the wind is blowing:

• Don't lob with a strong wind because balls can be carried out.
• Lobbing into the wind is a good tactic because balls blown about in the air are difficult to judge.
• Lobbing in the sun is also a good tactic. Fighting the sun is always difficult and will disturb your opponent's concentration.

## HOW TO PLAY IN THE WIND

If the wind is blowing while you are getting ready to serve, wait or bounce the ball a few extra times, and perhaps the wind will die for the moment you need to serve. If you must serve in the wind, toss the ball lower than normal and the wind will have less time to move it.

*With* the wind, hit groundstrokes hard and low over the net. *Against* the wind hit them high over the net to give the wind the opportunity to move the ball erratically and make it difficult to judge.

Do not lob *with* the wind because the ball can be easily carried out. Lob *against* the wind and your opponent will have a tough time judging it as the wind blows it about.

If the wind is blowing across the court, adjust your margin for error accordingly or the ball could be carried out. For example, if the wind is gusting to the right corner and you are planning to serve there, leave a bigger margin for error than usual. Serving to the left corner in this kind of a wind would be safer because, if the wind did take it, it would blow it *into* the service court rather than out. With side winds leave a large margin for error when hitting with the wind, a smaller one against it. Play your shots low over the net.

## HOW TO PLAY IN THE SUN

Whenever you play in the sun, be sure to place its position in your mind and hit shots that force your opponent to fight it.

Whenever you are forced to fight the sun, try to turn away from it.

Let lobs hit in the sun bounce before you hit an overhead.

Never look directly into the sun if you can avoid it. It could blind you momentarily.

## HOW TO PLAY WITH THE SUN GOING DOWN

To give yourself more time to judge the ball as the sunlight fades, move back gradually from your usual ready positions in keeping with the loss of visibility. Concentrate on trying to read the ball earlier and getting your racquet prepared sooner.

When you go in to the net, there's less time to read the ball and even a small loss of light can make a big difference. To make your volley, make your platform a little sooner than usual to gain more time to judge the ball. If you're making errors because of poor visibility, change your tactics before you give away the match.

On all your shots, wait longer before you hit and don't try to do as much.

# The Attacking Game Simplified

- **What It Takes**
- **Approach Shots**
- **Volley Tactics**
- **Overhead Tactics**

## What It Takes

Playing an attacking game requires an aggressive nature, the ability to make approach shots, volleys, and overheads, and the capability of putting the ball away when the opportunity occurs. You must be alert and ready to attack at every chance you get. You must attack short balls, when you drive your opponent out of position, and behind drop shots or chips. There are lots of opportunities to go to net. The number of short balls hit by average players is innumerable.

Program yourself before you play to be grimly determined not to miss any opportunities. Between points, program and reprogram yourself to jump on the first chance you get to go in. When you get that chance, have no fears. Attack! This is not a style of play for the faint of heart. Play bravely and you'll improve rapidly.

### WHY MAKE A PLATFORM?

Making a platform places you in a balanced position from which to judge and move to the ball. Learning to make this move is an important part of becoming a good net player.

Collected and Balanced Positions

## WHEN DO YOU MAKE A PLATFORM?

Whenever you approach the net, make a platform as your opponent hits. Now you're in the best position to read the ball and to get to it, no matter where your opponent hits to.

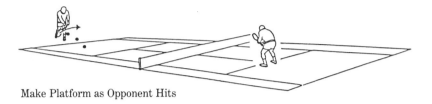

Make Platform as Opponent Hits

To be sure you have the time to make the platform, make it when your shot lands in your opponent's court and your opponent is in position to hit the ball. You will need the time it takes for the ball to bounce and be hit by your opponent to stop yourself and set up to hit. Like an automobile, you can't stop instantly. You need time to stop your momentum depending on your speed. BETTER TO STOP A LITTLE TOO SOON THAN TOO LATE.

## Approach Shots

### WHAT IS AN APPROACH SHOT?

An approach shot is any shot you hit that gives you the opportunity to get to net.

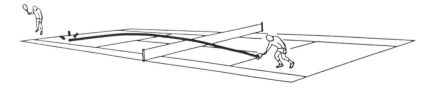

## HOW TO HIT AN APPROACH SHOT

If the ball is short, move alongside and through it. Hit without hesitation 1 ft or lower over the net, and hold your aimpoint. Keep moving forward as you hit, and follow the line of the shot in toward the net.

If you stop, then hit, by the time you get started again, it may be too late to get in position for the next shot.

On low balls very close to the net, chip or slice the approach carefully. Don't hit these shots flat or you'll make too many errors; and don't hit with topspin because it's too difficult to get the racquet far enough underneath the ball to brush it up over the net. Play these shots with tender loving care, but be definite with your follow-through.

## WHEN CAN YOU APPROACH THE NET?

Approach when your opponent hits a short ball you can attack.

Approach behind any deep, high bouncing shot that forces the opponent backwards to hit.

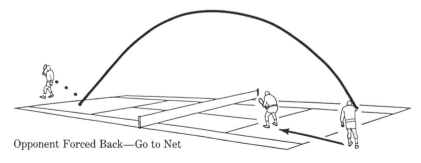

Opponent Forced Back—Go to Net

Approach behind a chip or drop shot just over the net near the sideline.

Approach behind any shot that forces your opponent backwards or off-balance.

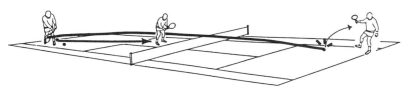

Approach behind a ball which lands at the feet of an opponent near the net. The return will be coming to you in an up trajectory and can be volleyed.

## WHERE TO HIT APPROACH SHOTS

Where to hit approach shots depends on your position in the court and your position to the ball.

Approach Shot Down The Line.

If the ball lands in your service court near the sideline, make the approach shot down the line. Hitting down the line gives you a shorter trip to net than going cross-court.

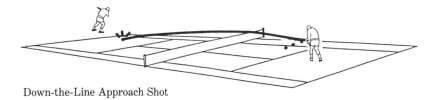

Down-the-Line Approach Shot

### Approach Shot Down The Center

If the ball lands near the "T", make the approach deep to the center mark.

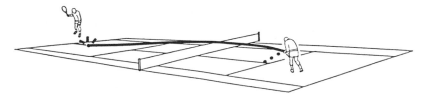

Down-the-Center Approach Shot

### Approach Shot Cross-Court

When you get to any short ball and your body is in an open hitting position, it's safer to make the approach shot cross-court.

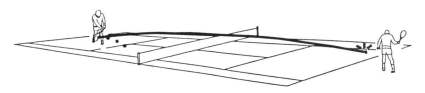

Open Hitting Position

### Approach Shot Hit Short

Hit the approach short to the service court sideline when your opponent is out of position deep behind the baseline.

Short Angle Shot

## WHERE TO MOVE AFTER YOU HIT THE APPROACH SHOT

After you make the approach shot, be sure to move to net so as to cut off the return.

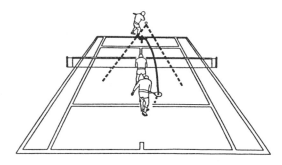

Down-the-Center

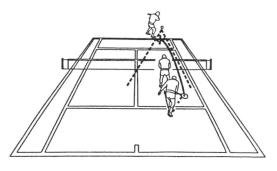

Down-the-Line

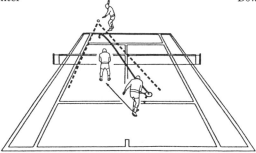

Cross-Court

You are now in position to hit a volley or an overhead.

## Volley Tactics

Always try to get as close to the net as possible and volley the ball as it's coming up. This is the easiest volley to make, and you have all kinds of aimpoints to choose from.

When the ball comes at you with tremendous speed, volley it back deep. It's too chancy to try to angle it and keep it in the court.

99

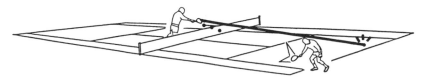

Hit Volley Deep

## ANGLE VOLLEYS

When close to the net, volley high balls at as sharp an angle as you can. The closer you are to the net, the sharper the angle you can use. Be sure to *start your stroke high above the ball* or you will be unable to angle it sharply. The *higher the racquet, the sharper the angle* you can make.

Hit the upper outside part of the ball, and hold your aimpoint.

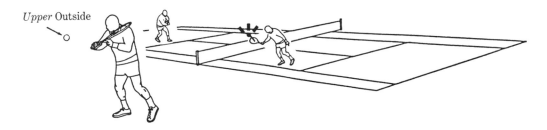

*Upper* Outside

Racquet Must Stop
at Top of Stroke

Don't do more than you have to do to win the point. A well-placed volley with a good margin of safety will win the point most of the time.

Always take the racquet back higher than the ball—*too high rather than too low*. If you take the racquet back high, you can still make a low volley because the natural action of your shoulder brings the racquet down swiftly without hesitation.

A racquet prepared too low, however, cannot usually be lifted and then swung forward in time because it must stop at the top of the stroke before it comes forward. (Try it.) There is just no time to do this in the face of a ball coming at you with any speed.

## LOW VOLLEYS

Try not to volley any ball below and close to the net. This is a tough volley to make and very defensive. Instead, whenever you can react quickly enough, step back and let the ball bounce; then move in as you hit and your shot can be more of an attacking shot rather than a defensive one.

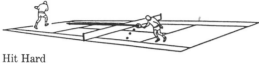

Hit Hard

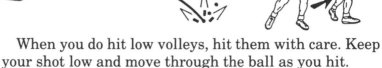

When you do hit low volleys, hit them with care. Keep your shot low and move through the ball as you hit.

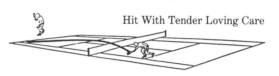

Hit With Tender Loving Care

## WIDE VOLLEYS

### IF THE BALL COMES WIDE, STAY WIDE.

Hit all volleys that you stretch or reach wide for *down the line*. Your racquet will stay on the ball longer and you'll have a better chance of keeping the shot in the court. If you try to hit cross-court, your racquet can easily pull off the ball, and the shot will slide wide or go into the net.

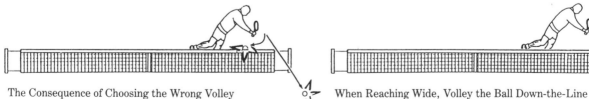

The Consequence of Choosing the Wrong Volley for Your Position to the Ball

When Reaching Wide, Volley the Ball Down-the-Line

When you're stretching out or reaching wide down the line, you're off balance. There is usually no way to recover to take a return shot. Therefore, this is your last shot of that point. GO FOR IT! Hit down the line and try to *put the ball away*.

## HIGH SWINGING VOLLEYS

If you are in good position for a slow, high ball and you feel like running through it and taking a big swing to knock the ball away, go ahead and do it! Nothing you do is wrong if you make the shot. What difference does the size of the swing make if you win the point? Everyone likes to try for a spectacular shot from time to time.

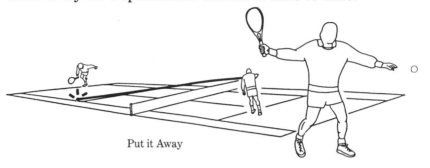

Put it Away

However, don't be foolish and get carried away just because you've occasionally made a great shot. You won't become a good volleyer if you snap your wrist or take a big swing on every volley.

## Overhead Tactics

When you are close to the net, aim your overhead at a sharp angle. Midway to a sideline in the service court is a terrific shot.

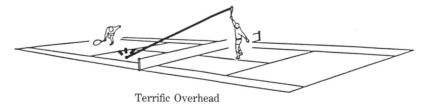

Terrific Overhead

On lobs which move you back deep, hit your overheads preferably up the backhand sideline at as much of an

angle as your depth in the court permits. The further from the net you are, the smaller your angle, and the deeper you must hit.

If the ball is past your hitting area and behind your head, roll or snap your racquet more quickly than when you take the ball in your normal hitting area. Otherwise, the "cover" won't get over the ball to keep it in the court.

Let very high balls which push you back deep—or which you're not in position to hit—bounce. When hitting an overhead on a ball that bounces, the tendency is to hit short or in the net. To correct this, aim for the baseline. Hold the baseline in your mind as you hit. This will compel your racquet to hit out through the ball. Aim preferably to your opponent's backhand.

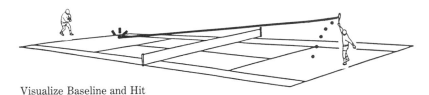

Visualize Baseline and Hit

Hit Deep Overheads from this Position

If it still goes in the net or lands short, aim the next one to the opponent's back fence. Don't worry, the ball will rarely go out, it will just land deep in the opponent's court. The reason that you needn't be concerned about hitting the back fence or hitting the ball out is that most average players lack the ability to hit an overhead that far without having the ball bounce. You won't hit the fence 5% of the time. Try it.

When you hit overheads, don't give any quarter. Destroy the ball. You should win the point every time. If your opponent returns the ball, you did something wrong. Either you didn't place the ball correctly or you didn't hit it hard enough. Your opponent should never be able to return the ball.

# The Serve and Volley Game Simplified

- **Net Coverage**
- **The Service Toss**
- **The Serve**
- **Volley Tactics**
- **Volley Tactic Tips**

# Net Coverage

If you want to be a serve and volley player, you must be aggressive, agile, and fast. Strong serves, volleys, and overheads are the essential tools of a serve and volley player. You must become a very astute tennis strategist.

*You can't cover the entire net.* For the most part, you can cover a couple of steps to the right or left of your net position. It's crucial therefore to know where your opponent is most likely to hit the ball and to place yourself in the center of the area of probable returns.

## HOW TO COVER THE AREA OF PROBABLE RETURNS

If you volley to the right or left baseline corners, move to the center of the service court and close to the net to cover the return shot. From that position, you can cover the down-the-line return or the cross-court. It will take a great angle shot or lob to get by you.

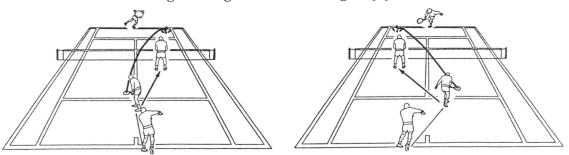

Move to Center of Service Court—Close to Net

Cut off angle shots *by moving diagonally* in toward the net. The sharper the angle of the shot, the straighter you must move in to cut it off.

Visualize your hitting area. Don't think about hitting the ball. *Think about moving through the ball* and of *where you want to hit the volley.* These are acquired talents. They are man-made and require deliberate thought until they are thoroughly programmed. *Swinging at a ball that is coming at you is instinctive because the ball is*

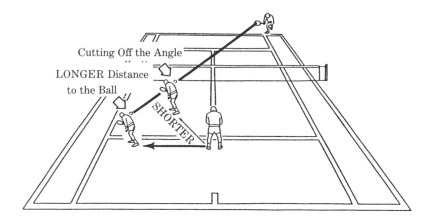

Cutting Off the Angle

LONGER Distance
to the Ball

SHORTER

*first a projectile.* It's natural to brush it away. You don't have to think about hitting. You'll hit when it's time to hit.

If you volley down the center *move to the center of the net* to cover the returns.

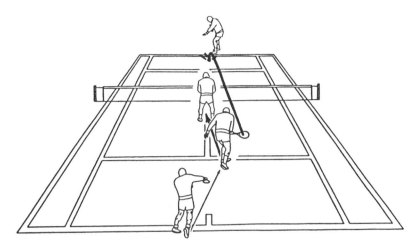

Move to the Center of the Net

## The Service Toss

Toss the ball as far out in front of you as is consistent with your ability to serve effectively. The further out into the court you can toss the ball, the further into the court you will be after you've served. This is a great plus in getting closer to the net for your first volley.

○  Toss Ball out in Front of You

## The Serve

Don't try to serve aces. The added pressure makes the risks of your serve breaking up much greater. Let the aces happen because they happen. Serve the ball within a frame where you feel confident. Analyze your opponent's ability to return. If you are playing a new opponent, explore his or her capabilities. *Serve to different places in the service court.* Try whatever serves are in your arsenal. Don't serve closer to your maximum than is required to draw an error or a defensive return that you can volley. Move in behind your serve and make a platform as your serve bounces in the opponent's service court. (See p. 95.)

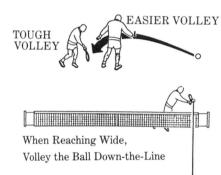

## Volley Tactics

Try to take every volley in an up trajectory. Meet the ball coming up and as close to the net as you can get. The sharper the angle at which you want to hit, the higher you must prepare the racquet above the ball.

When reaching wide for a ball, think of hitting the outside of the ball and volley down the line. (See p. 101.)

If you take your first volley near the "T" and your body is open, volley cross-court to the baseline corners.

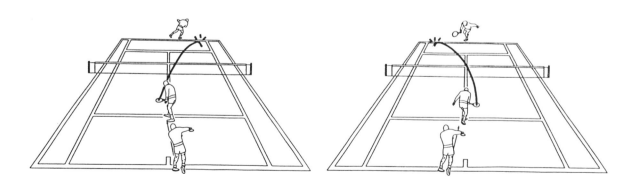

Open Hitting Position—Volley Cross-Court

Don't volley down the line from an open position. Volleying the ball from this position increases your incidence of error because your racquet will contact the inside part of the ball. You will volley inside-out and the ball is more apt to slide off the strings and send the ball into the net or out the sidelines. (See p. 82.)

Even if you make the volley, it won't be as effective as your cross-court volley. It will be a slower, spinning volley that gives your opponent more time to get to it. From an open position, you can volley more naturally and solidly cross-court than down the line. Try it.

Stand in an open position and press your hand out cross-court. Then press your hand down the line. You'll feel the difference.

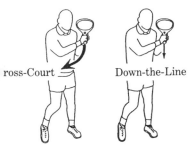
ross-Court     Down-the-Line

## Volley Tactic Tips

1. Don't volley inside-out unless you are volleying from a position that gives you a lot of room in your opponent's court to shoot into. Play always with the thought of making your opponent hit the ball to make a point. Don't give away free points by making errors.

2. When reaching wide for a ball, volley down the line and think of hitting the outside of the ball. It will induce you to stretch further for the ball and you will get better hold of it. This will prevent the volley from sliding out the sideline.

3. Angle high volleys. Start your volley stroke from above the ball. The higher you get your racquet above the ball, the sharper angle volley you can make.

4. Volley all low balls low over the net. Volley low balls close to the net with tender, loving care. Get down to the height of the ball and stay down until you have completed the volley.

5. For balls that you volley above the net, put them away for the point. Don't be weak. Destroy the ball. Obliterate it. It will give you confidence.

# Serving Tactics Simplified

- **Serving Into the Body**
- **Quick Serving**
- **Faulting**
- **Lining Up To Serve**

In a match don't try to serve to places that you are not accustomed to. You can't expect good results if you do. The best tactic is to hit to places to which you can hit confidently and accurately.

Too often players make the mistake of sacrificing their best serves in their eagerness to try to exploit their opponent's weaknesses. Serve to a weakness only if you can do it well enough to force an error or draw a defensive return. Otherwise forget it, or your own game will suffer.

*Never change your serve just for the sake of changing.* For example, if you are serving to your opponent's backhand corner and drawing errors or weak returns, why change? Keep serving there. Serving to the same place time after time will increase your confidence as the match progresses and will make your serve more and more grooved. It may also damage your opponent's morale. *There's no reason to change your serve until your opponent begins to hurt you with the return.* Only then do you have a reason to change tactics and vary your serves.

The most sophisticated use of the serve is the ability to vary the serves you're capable of making. Serve to different places in the service courts to prevent your opponent from getting set.

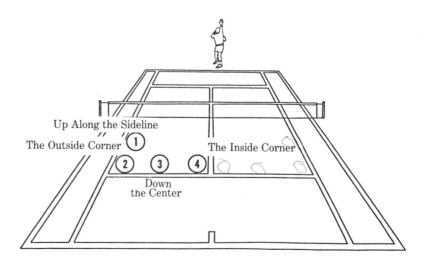

*reasons why* [handwritten]

## Serving Into the Body

*(1) helps against big players* [handwritten]
*(2) helps against stand in players* [handwritten]
*(3) helps to give into when going to net* [handwritten]

Serve into players who are big because they will have trouble getting their bodies out of the way. Serve also into players who stand inside the baseline to receive your serve or who attack your serve by moving into it.

When you're going to net behind your serve, serving into your opponent's body cuts down the angle of return, making it more difficult for the receiver to pass you when jammed by the ball. It's hard for the receiver to move out of the way and make a good return. Going in behind your serve also exerts enormous pressure on the receiver and increases your chances of getting a poor return.

*less time for ball to get to returner* [handwritten]

## Quick Serving

*why – helps when being hurt against K.S.* [handwritten]

*Toss lower, in front of you – move in* [handwritten]

Quick serving is a good change and a good tactic when being hurt by the return. Just toss the ball lower and more in front of you than usual. It's more difficult for the receiver to read a quick serve because the toss is in the air a shorter time and you hit more quickly.

---

*Playing tip*    Use this difficult quick serving technique only if you are an advanced player and use it only on days when your timing and rhythm are especially good.

---

## Faulting

*Be sure to correct the (action) program errors in your mind immediately.* [handwritten]

When you fault, be sure to correct the program in your mind. On the next serve, concentrate only on making the needed correction.

If your first serve isn't working on a given day, don't be stubborn and keep using it in the hope that it will get better. It probably won't. Use your second serve. You'll have a better chance of getting your timing and rhythm back. After several games, try your first serve again; perhaps now it will work. If it doesn't, go back to your second serve. See Rules for correcting service faults, p. 182.

## Lining Up To Serve

*Right-Handed Servers* ( ½ way — can move

When serving into the *deuce* court, stand next to the center mark, for the following reasons.

(1) From "x," you can serve over the lowest part of the net to the inside corner of the service court. This means that you can hit to a right-handed player's backhand with less risk of faulting into the net.

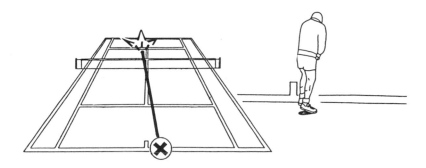

(2) From next to the center mark you are as close as possible to your aimpoint. The shorter the distance your serve has to travel, the less time your opponent has to react.

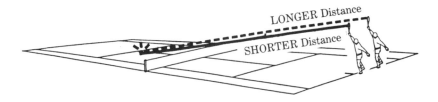

Baseline Ready Position

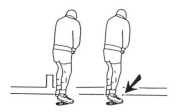

(3) For baseline tennis, a ready position from behind the center mark is the best place from which to cover the court. From a service position next to the center mark, you'll remain close to it after serving. Don't line up too far to the right of the center mark because you turn away from it as you serve. The farther you move away from it, the harder it is to get back behind it for the next shot.

When serving to the *ad* court, stand *about 3 feet to the left of the center mark for 2 reasons:*

(1) From there you can serve over a lower part of the net to the outside corner. Serving from closer to the center mark would mean *serving over a higher part of the net,* increasing the chance of error and making it more difficult to place the serve at an angle to the sideline.

Stand 3 ft from the Center Mark

(2) You can afford to line up a few feet to the left of the center mark because *from this side your body will turn in toward the center* as you serve. From this position you are only a step away from the center mark after serving and can get behind it quickly in order to be ready for the service return.

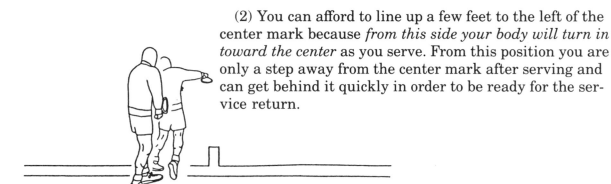

*Left-Handed Servers*

When left-handers serve to the *deuce* court, they *turn in toward the center* as they serve. They should line up about 3 feet to the right of the center mark and closer to the center mark when serving to the ad court because they *turn away from the center.* Basically the reasons are the reverse of those given for right-handed servers.

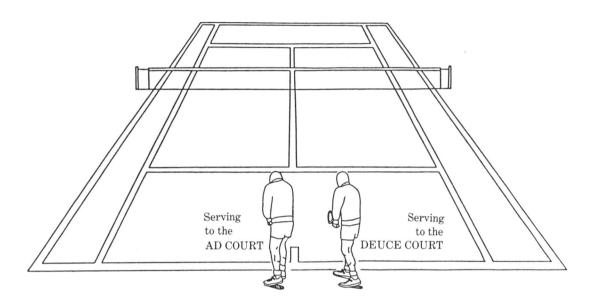

Serving to the AD COURT

Serving to the DEUCE COURT

# The Return of Serve Simplified

- **Take the Serve Away From the Server**

- **Program Yourself To Return Serve**

- **What Kind of Stroke To Use**

- **Where To Stand To Return Serve**

- **What To Do as the Server Makes the Toss**

*Give yourself a chance to play some tennis.*
*Don't keep knocking your returns Out!*

## Take the Serve Away From the Server

The best tactic on the return of serve is to take the serve away from the server by playing the ball back safely. Once the serve has been returned, the advantage of serving has been lost and you are now playing the point on an even basis. Think of what this does to your opponent psychologically.

The effect can be devastating if you keep getting the serve back. It means that all of the work put into the development of the serve has been to no avail against *you*. Many players' egos will react by trying to serve harder and harder until eventually they begin to crack and fault. Once their serves break down, the rest of their game is likely to fall apart as well.

On the other hand, every time you miss the return, you make your opponent more confident. Knocking returns out by trying to hit winners doesn't give you a chance to play much tennis and your opponent doesn't have to do much to hold his serve. Why try to do so much? If your mind is always pressured by thoughts of making the point, too little of your concentration is on making the return.

Return the serve at a speed that you feel confident will keep the ball in the court. This will put more pressure on your opponent, who now has to play some tennis to win a point. Your confidence will build as you make more returns, and your returns will get better and better without any extra effort to improve them.

Although you should always try to return serve safely, this does not mean tentatively. Be very definite and authoritative whenever you swing no matter how softly or hard you're hitting. Never pull (restrict) a stroke once you've decided to swing. Hitting through the ball is what causes the strings to form a pocket that will hold the ball on the racquet longer.

### *Examples*

(1) If your opponent serves and stays at the baseline, aim the ball with a good margin of safety above the net to a point deep in your opponent's court.

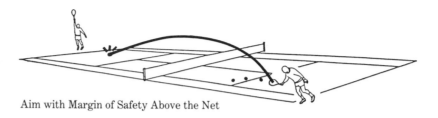

Aim with Margin of Safety Above the Net

(2) If the server is coming in, don't let it rush you. Aim your shots lower over the net. Put all your concentration into aiming the return at your opponent's feet or making a passing shot. Don't get too chancy. Hit a return that you feel sure you can make.

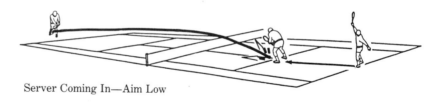

Server Coming In—Aim Low

(3) The best shot against a net-rusher, if you have the stroke, is a low topspin drive. A spinning ball that's dipping lower than the net is tough to volley.

Low Topspin Drive

(4) Lobbing your return will make a net-rusher more hesitant about getting in too close to the net.

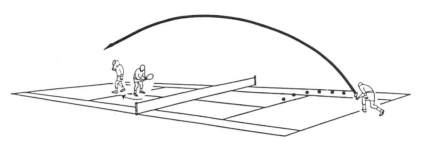

Lob Net-Rushers

## Program Yourself to Return Serve

Take advantage of the stop in play before each serve to *program yourself to return serve.* Once the serve is hit, there's very little time to decide where and how to return serve. You should think about it *before* the serve is hit.

The first thing to do is to visualize the various places in the service court the serve may be hit. (See the illustrations below.) The serve can be hit to any of these places or anywhere in between.

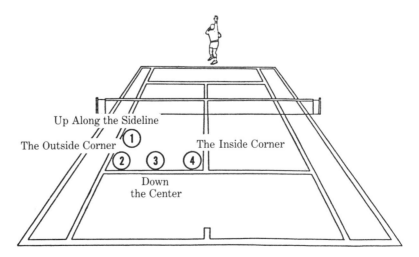

Up Along the Sideline

The Outside Corner

The Inside Corner

Down the Center

## RETURNING SERVES HIT TO THE AD COURT

Return ball #1 down the line to the corner. Because the serve has pulled you so wide out of the court, the chances are that you won't get far enough behind the ball to hit it cross-court. Even if you do manage to hit it cross-court, unless you hit a winner, you have left your forehand side wide open and your opponent can put the ball away.

Return Serve Down-the-Line

Return balls #2 and #3 with your backhand deep down the center or cross-court. The advantage of taking ball #3 on your backhand is that as you swing you are moving toward the center which is where you want to be for your next shot. However, if you lack the ability to do this because of a weak backhand, then by all means take this ball with your forehand.

Return Serve Down-the-Center or Cross-Court

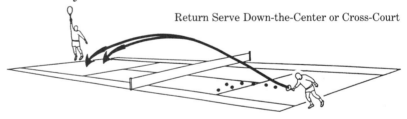

Return ball #4 with your forehand deep down the line, to the center, or cross-court.

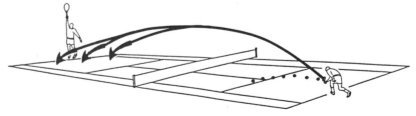

Return Serve Down-the-Center, Cross-Court, or Down-the-Line

## RETURNING SERVES HIT TO THE DEUCE COURT

Return ball #1 down the line to the corner. Because the serve has pulled you wide out of the court, the chances are that you won't get far enough behind the ball to hit it cross-court. Even if you do manage to hit it cross-court, unless you hit a winner, you have left your backhand side wide open, and your opponent can put the ball away.

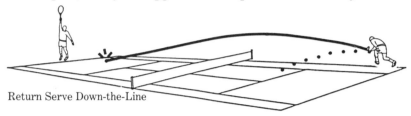

Return Serve Down-the-Line

Return balls #2 and #3 with your forehand deep down the center or cross-court deep to the sideline. In order to take ball #3 on your forehand, you may have to run around it. *The advantage of taking this ball on your forehand* is that, as you swing, you are moving toward the center of the court, which is where you want to be to cover the next shot. Do not try to hit ball #3 down the line. *You can easily make an error because you'll be hitting inside out from an open position and the ball can slide off the racquet.*

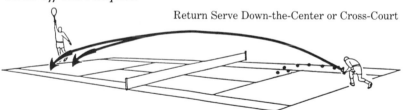

Return Serve Down-the-Center or Cross-Court

Return ball #4 with your backhand deep down the line, down the center, or cross-court.

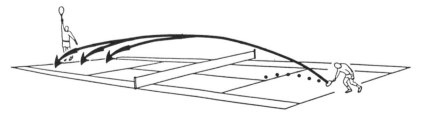

## What Kind of Stroke To Use

Try to use your full strokes to return serve. If the serve is a real bomb or you are late in judging it, shorten your backswing in order to meet the ball. If you have a drive and a slice on both sides, drive all serves that come at speeds you can handle, and slice all serves that are troublesome. If you're not making the returns, lob.

*No matter which stroke you use, be sure to step into the ball* and hold your aimpoint. Otherwise, the racquet strings may not form a pocket big enough to take good hold of the ball.

## Where To Stand To Return Serve

Against powerful serves, stand back behind the baseline as far as necessary to make safe returns.

If you move better to your right than to your left or if you have a better stroke on one side than the other, give yourself a break by edging a little to the weaker side. Experience will show you how far over you can go before hurting your return on the other side.

Against a server who is grooved to hitting to the backhand corners, move toward them a bit. This may induce the server to hit to places he or she is not as confident with and increase the chances of drawing a fault.

Against a slice serve that curves away from you, be mentally prepared to take an extra step or half-step to move behind it to get a good hold of the ball. This will prevent the ball from sliding off the racquet and ensure a good hit. If the server is slicing into your backhand side, take a side step away from it or make the return with your forehand.

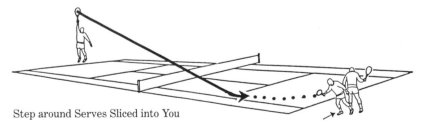

Step around Serves Sliced into You

Against a spin serve, *move in and take the ball on the way up before it breaks away from you.* If you don't have the capacity to do this, stand back and *let the ball come over the top of the bounce and fall* before you swing. Then hit under and through the ball. The key is to stand in the best place to make a safe return.

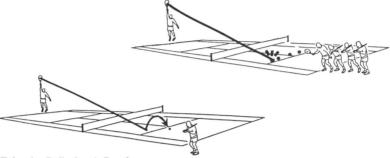

Take the Ball after it Breaks

Against a weak serve, stand in closer to receive. Move in alongside the ball. Use your full forehand or backhand stroke. Hold an aimpoint and try to put the return away for the point.

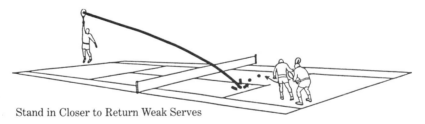

Stand in Closer to Return Weak Serves

## What To Do as the Server Makes the Toss

The return of serve is a tough, critical shot. If you can't return serve, you can't play. Without a planned method of returning, it's even more difficult. While programming yourself to return serve only takes a few seconds, it requires great concentration and an iron will to do it before each and every serve.

Crouch

Best Position to Hold Racquet

Program yourself to:

Crouch and stay forward on the balls of your feet. You are more alert when you crouch than when you stand upright.

Hold the racquet centered in front of you. It's now equidistant to either side. It can be taken back to your forehand or backhand without wasted time. If you hold your racquet to one side of your body, and the ball is served to the other, the extra time it takes to get the racquet back can make the difference as to whether or not you make the return.

Do not look at the swing of your opponent's racquet. Fluky swings are very distracting. *Train your eyes on the ball in your opponent's hand and never allow your eyes to leave it as it is tossed.* If you fail to keep your eyes on the ball and don't pick it up until after it's served, there won't be much time left to judge it. This will make it very difficult to make a return. The *time lag between starting to judge the ball as it is tossed and after it's been hit can spell the difference between making a good return, a poor return, or no return at all.*

Bounce lightly as the ball is tossed. If you're standing flat-footed, making that first step into the ball takes "forever" in relation to the speed of the serve. Too much time is lost in lifting and throwing your weight forward to start to move.

Don't hold your breath while waiting to return serve or your insides will tighten. Relax by breathing easily and naturally.

Hold the racquet gently and don't tighten the grip until you hit.

Keep your body free and keep your mind fixed on making the return.

Start your racquet back by pivoting your shoulders as soon as you read the ball. Pivoting your shoulders is a faster way to get the racquet back than just swinging your arm. Try it!

Pivot Shoulders to get Racquet Back

Be sure to move your shoulders first, not your feet. If the ball is on you and your racquet isn't back, you have nothing with which to hit. Watch the bounce of the ball. Try to see the ball hit the ground, or it will be more difficult to read the speed and direction of the ball.

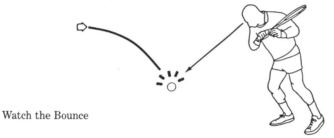

Watch the Bounce

Step in, aim, and hit. Moving into the shot forces the strings to form a pocket and holds the ball on the racquet longer. This increases your chance of delivering an accurate and powerful service return. (See p. 62.) The harder the serve, the more important it is that you force yourself to move into the ball. Players fail to pivot and step forward because they're afraid that they don't have time to do it. However, there's always time if you compel yourself to take it.

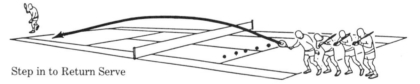

Step in to Return Serve

*Whatever else you forget to do, don't forget to hold your aimpoint* until you have completed the return! Remember: your stroke will collapse the moment you drop the aimpoint from your mind.

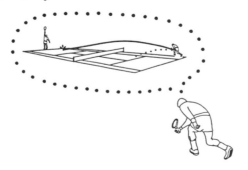

# Programming Simplified

- **Match Preparation**
- **Continue To Program Between Points**
- **Develop Your Own Programs**
- **Match Preparation for Tournaments**

# Match Preparation

Never walk out on a tennis court without having programmed what you are going to do. Good mental preparation increases your chances of playing your best. Before going out to practice or play, take a few minutes to sit quietly by yourself. If you don't plan before going out to play, when are you going to do it? Certainly there's not much time to do it once the balls come flying at you.

*A Sample Program*

Visualize:

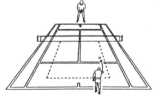

Your position behind the center mark at the baseline and the margin for error you need. Staying mobile. Bouncing lightly on the balls of your feet as your opponent hits.

Keeping your body free by thinking and feeling yourself relaxed. If you start to tighten up inside, exhale forcefully. This will help you relax.

3 to 8 Feet Over the Net

Hitting under every ball from the baseline, no matter how high or low the bounce.

Hitting from the baseline 3 to 8 ft (or more) over the net, and keeping the ball deep.

Hitting most shots cross-court.

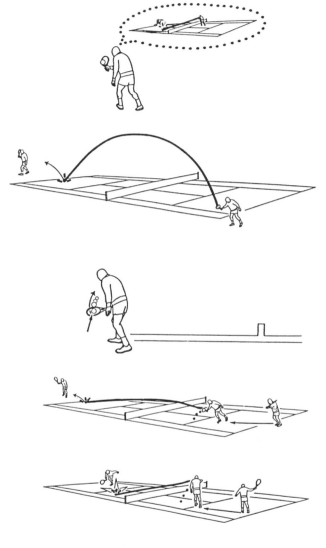

Holding your aimpoints firmly in your mind throughout every shot no matter what else you fail to do.

Lobbing the ball high and deep to the center mark. Think of hitting at 2 mph whenever you are moving backward or out of position.

Thinking of hitting the outside part of the ball as you move toward the sideline.

Moving in on every short ball and hitting 1 ft or lower over the net.

Moving in on a short ball bouncing higher than the net and putting it away for the point.

Your opponent's weaknesses and decide how to exploit them. Plan the tactics and the plays you are going to use. Include how you're going to handle your own weaknesses. For example, run around your backhand if your forehand is stronger. Play your strongest shots as often as you can, and serve only to the places you're most grooved to.

Play within your capabilities. Place yourself within a playing frame where you feel comfortable, and stay there. Don't ask yourself to do things beyond your limits. If you do, you'll just throw the match away.

## Continue To Program Between Points

Program yourself in between points as much as you can.

When your opponent is serving and has just a few feet to walk to get the balls, you don't have much time for programming anything other than how you plan to return serve. If, however, your opponent has to walk a long distance to two different parts of the court to get the balls, then you have a lot of time to reprogram yourself.

The most difficult part of reprogramming yourself is that you must think repeatedly of the same things over and over again like a broken record. From time to time you may hear a TV announcer indicate a player is "zapped out" from a tough five-set match the previous day. It isn't the physical effort that "zaps out" players as much as the strain to maintain their concentration throughout the match that wears them out.

*Don't think about winning the match. Concentrate on trying to win each point.* (The points win games, games win sets, and sets win matches.)

Don't worry about *who* your opponent is. All you can do is play the best that you can; so there's no point in worrying about who you're up against.

## Develop Your Own Programs

Many players are programmed just the opposite of the way they should be. They generally think first and foremost of hitting the ball. *Their first thoughts should be to get in position with their racquets prepared to hit.* The last thing to think about is hitting the tennis ball.

# Match Preparation for Tournaments

Everything you do to prepare for a tournament match should be something to build confidence and decrease anxiety. Here are some of the things you can do:

*Fitness:* Stay in good physical shape. Don't let anyone run you into the ground. It's a terrible way to lose. Don't change your sleeping pattern. Don't change your diet.

*Body Chemistry:* Don't change your regular routine. You'll have a better chance to play your best if your metabolism is not disturbed. When possible, play as close to the time of day when you normally play.

*Clothing:* Go into a match turned out well. Don't wear anything new or binding. Particularly, don't wear new shoes. New shoes are less comfortable than old ones and they are heavier because the soles haven't been worn down. Even an ounce can make a big difference in your speed. Race horses are shod with light-weight shoes to keep their feet close to the ground when they run. Fractions of an ounce make a difference in their speed. The heavier your shoes, the harder it is to lift them. Wear your old shoes as long as the traction is good. Like a race horse, the heavier your shoes the slower you move.

*Practice:* Don't leave your tennis game on the practice court by overdoing your practice just before a match. Practice the way you are planning to play. Work more on the strong parts of your game. It's important to feel confident about what you do best. You can't improve your weaknesses enough in just a few hours to be of much help in a match.

*Programming:* Remember, anxiety stems from uncertainty. Good preparation before you play will make you less anxious because you'll know what you want to do.

---

***Playing tip***    Don't watch any matches before you play. You can look at just so many tennis balls before you start to lose concentration. You don't want to leave your game in the stands.

# Doubles Simplified

- **The Doubles Game Versus the Singles Game**

- **Playing Positions**

- **Keep Your Doubles Play Simplified**

- **More Tactics**

- **How To Return Serve**

- **How To Serve**

- **Doubles Tips**

## The Doubles Game Versus the Singles Game

*The Sameness in the Games*

Playing doubles is generally considered a totally different game from singles. This is an incorrect interpretation. Let's take a look at the playing tactics of both and compare them.

***Example 1*** Playing Tactic—*Singles*
When returning serve against a serve and volley player, you would *aim the ball low over the net or lob.*

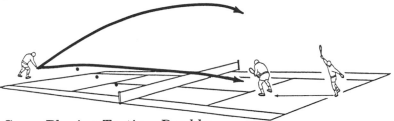

Same Playing Tactic—*Doubles*
How would you return the serve in the same playing situation in doubles? You would make the return *in exactly the same way.*

***Example 2*** Playing Tactic—*Singles*
If you are returning serve against a player who stays at the baseline, you would *return the ball at a good, safe height over the net and aim it deep to the baseline.*

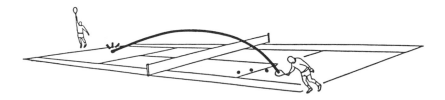

Same Playing Tactic—*Doubles*

How would you make the return in the same playing situation in doubles? If the player at the net is incapable of poaching,* *you would make the same return.*

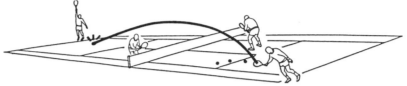

***Example 3*** Playing Tactic—*Singles and Doubles*

Let's suppose now that you don't have the skills to execute the tactics defined. What should you do? *You should make the shot that you are surest of making* without regard to where your opponents are. Give your opponents the chance of making an error rather than risk making one by trying to make shots beyond your capabilities.

***Example 4*** Playing Tactic—*Singles*

When you go to the net behind your serve or any other shot, *you would try to put away any shots you can take above the net* by hitting to the open part of the court. *Shots that you take below the net, you would volley low and deep or at an angle to the court.*

Same Playing Tactic—*Doubles*

How would you handle these same shots if you were playing doubles? *You would handle them the same way you did in singles.*

*To cross over into your partner's side of the court to hit the ball.

***Example 5*** Same Playing Tactics—Singles and Doubles

1. When you hit against a player at the baseline, you would generally hit shots high over the net with a big safety margin and *hit deep to the baseline*.

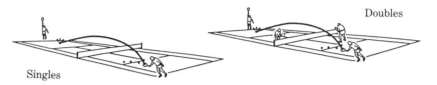

Doubles

Singles

2. If your opponent was *out of position,* then you would *hit hard and low* to the part of the court that was open for a winner.

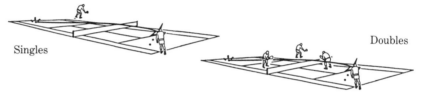

Doubles

Singles

3. When you are in an uncomfortable hitting position, you would *throw the ball back*.

Doubles

Singles

4. Against players coming into the net, you would *hit low balls*.

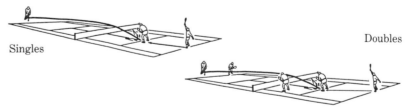

Doubles

Singles

5. When you move in to take a short ball and your opponent is at the net, you would *hit low shots into your opponent, lob, or hit a passing shot*.

**6.** If you are at the net, you would *angle your volleys or hit deep,* depending on your ability to handle the speed of the shot.

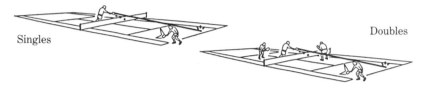

**7.** You would *hit overheads hard* to open spaces in the court.

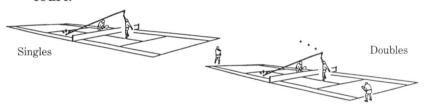

As you can see from these examples, the tactics that you would use to handle these situations are the same whether you are playing singles or doubles.

*These examples illustrate clearly the sameness between the singles game and the doubles game.* There is no need to play doubles any differently than you play singles. *Everything that you have learned in this course applies to doubles as well as singles.*

## Playing Positions

Many average players blindly follow the styles of play of other players. This is done at the cost of their playing abilities and the enjoyment of their game. I've asked some of these players why they play from their court positions. Their replies are (1) that's where everyone stands or (2) that's where you are supposed to stand.

Don't get trapped by what other players do. Be influenced only by your capabilities. There is just one place in the tennis court from which you are supposed to play. *That position is where you can play the best.*

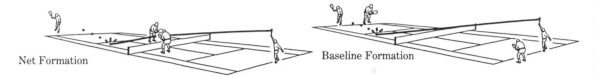

Net Formation                    Baseline Formation

On tennis courts everywhere players can be seen playing from positions that they are ill-equipped to handle. A prime example of this is to observe some of the tennis players who are playing at the net or from other positions in the service boxes. Most of them have no volley or overhead skills. In addition, they don't have the agility, the reflexes, or the knowledge of how to cover their net position. *They rarely go for a shot or get one that they can play. Their participation in the game is relatively nil. For most part, they stand and watch the other players hit the ball.* The result is that their partner is either playing both of their opponents or playing singles with one of them. At the end of each point they switch to the opposite side of the court and repeat this process until the match is over. *If you are one of these players, change your methods of playing.* There's no pleasure in being ineffectual and not participating in the match.

If your forehand and backhand strokes are your strongest weapons, play from a position that gives you the best opportunities to use them. *Your team should use a baseline formation to start every point whether it is serving or receiving serve.*

The next time you watch the world-class players playing doubles, note their positions in the court. When they are not playing well from net positions, they move back to a baseline formation. *There is no hesitation on their part in moving from one playing position to another.*

## Keep Your Doubles Play Simplified

*Cover your half of the tennis court* and leave the other half for your partner to cover.

Never poach unless you are sure you can win the point. *Poach only on shots that you can take above the net.*

*It's essential to stay bouncy or mobile* throughout every point. This is very difficult and takes a lot of fortitude. It's especially difficult if you go through a number of points without getting a chance to hit.

Aim all your shots inside the singles sideline. Use the singles sidelines as your margin for error.

Whenever you are uncertain about what to do, *lob.* (Review the lesson on the lob.)

*Play the shots you are surest of making.* If you have a better forehand stroke than backhand, *run around your backhand shots* and hit with your forehand whenever possible.

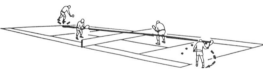

## More Tactics

*ATTACK!* That's the thought that should prevail in your mind from the beginning of a match to the end of it. This does not mean you should try to blast every ball. It means you should keep moving in steadily on every ball and take it as soon as possible. *The sooner you take the ball and the lower over the net you hit it, the less time there is for your opponent to get to it.* Whenever you hit a ball that is above the net, it should be put away. *You should win the point every time.* If you don't, you have done something wrong. *Either you didn't hit it with sufficient power or the placement wasn't good enough.* It doesn't make any difference how great a get your opponent makes. It's not supposed to happen.

*Always cover the center areas of the court.* This leaves your opponent the higher parts of the net to hit over and the smaller areas that are left along the sidelines to shoot for. These are chancy shots that carry a large incidence of error.

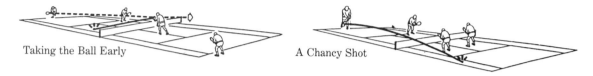

Taking the Ball Early    A Chancy Shot

*Volleys*

If you volley down the center and pull your opponent to the center, *volley the next ball to the sidelines* or reverse the play by hitting first to the sidelines, *then hit down the center.*

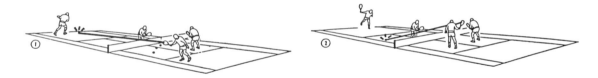

If you hit at your opponent's feet, your opponent must hit the ball in an up trajectory. Be prepared to move forward and volley the ball as it is coming up. Your partner at the net may also find it opportune to poach.

Whenever you or your partner hit a forcing shot*, move in close to the net.

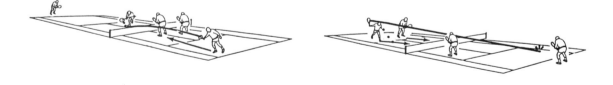

*A shot that presses your opponent.

When both teams are at the net, hit very low cross-court shots. Attack all shots you can take above the net.

When you are hitting from the baseline against a team with one player at the net and one back at the baseline, *don't hit to the net player.*

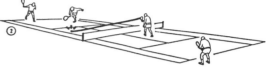

*The Consequence Of Hitting To The Net Player*

When you hit a shot *that forces your opponents to run back* for the ball, *go up to the net like a race horse.* When your opponent is about to hit, make a platform, then volley or hit an overhead.

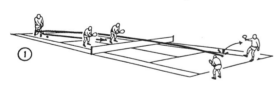

When you get a short ball, move in on the ball and *keep moving as you hit and go to the net.*

Keep Moving as You Hit

## How To Return Serve

Review Return Of Serve, pp. 117–125.

When returning serve against a serve and volley player, *hit the return low and cross-court.*

Return the serve down the line when you are pulled wide.

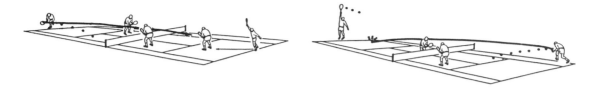

Don't rush the service return, but move in and take it as soon as possible. If you're having trouble making a good service return, lob it.

## How To Serve

Review Serving Tactics, pp. 111–115, and Faulting, p. 182.

Serve from a position *about* halfway between the center mark and the doubles baseline corner.

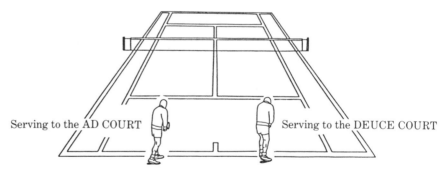

Serving to the AD COURT                    Serving to the DEUCE COURT

A serve to either of the inside corners of the service court restricts the angle of the service return. This makes it easier for you to cover the service return and lessens your opponent's chances of hitting a winner.

A serve into the body will often jam your opponent and prevent an offensive return.

A serve into the center of the right or left service court will bring the return back cross-court.

A serve delivered wide to either service court will often bring a return down the line.

## Doubles Tips

The stronger server on your team should serve first. If your team is playing from a net formation, the server should serve, volley, and get to the net. If your team is playing from a baseline formation, the server should stay at the baseline.

*Doubles teams should move together: backwards, forwards, and sideways to cover the court.*

The better playing member of a doubles team should cover the left or ad court. Then, when the opposing team is serving, the server will be faced with serving to the strongest member of your team at most of the crucial points of the game.

The size of the doubles court that each player is required to cover is 175½ square feet smaller than the singles court. This makes doubles a faster game to play than the singles game. With less court to cover, doubles players get to the ball more quickly and hit it sooner than players in a singles match. When both teams are at the net and volleying the ball at one another, it requires great reflexes and experience to judge the ball and respond to it.

Don't try to play outside your capabilities. Try to play within a frame that allows you to use your skills comfortably and efficiently.

If you have a good lob, use it frequently. If your forehand is better than your backhand, take every shot you can with it. Stay mobile throughout every point. *Do whatever you do best,* and you'll derive the maximum enjoyment out of your tennis game.

# The Forehand and Backhand Strokes Simplified

- **Forehand Versus Backhand**
- **The Forehand and Backhand Grips**
- **Your Hitting Areas**
- **How To Make a Forehand and Backhand Stroke**
- **The Forehand and Backhand Topspin Strokes**
- **The Forehand and Backhand Slice Strokes**

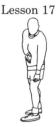

**FOREHAND STROKE**
Stroke is Blocked

**BACKHAND STROKE**
Stroke is Free

Stroke making causes more anguish and occupies more of the time of the average player than any other part of the game. Some players envision so many difficulties about the making of strokes that it would almost take some voodoo magic to produce them correctly. These difficulties are generated by mistaken beliefs about strokes.

## Forehand Versus Backhand

It's generally believed that the backhand stroke is harder to learn and harder to make than the forehand stroke. This is not true. *The forehand is far more difficult* because it requires bigger adjustments of your body.

When turned sideways on the forehand, your body is *in front of* the stroke, blocking the forward swing. If you weigh 165 pounds, that's 165 pounds you have to move out of the way in order to complete a forehand stroke. It's essential to be constantly aware of this whenever you are using your forehand. You must get your body out of the way of your stroke.

This problem does not exist on your backhand stroke. Your body is *in back of* the stroke and not in the way. Your arm is free to make the stroke. Don't be handicapped by the misconception that the backhand is harder.

To develop a good backhand stroke you need to: (1) get accustomed to performing from an unfamiliar side of your body, (2) understand the technique required to produce the stroke, and (3) *be aware of the similarities between forehand and backhand stroke production.*

## The Forehand and Backhand Grips

Hold the racquet balanced in your left hand. Your right hand should *hold a relaxed grip.* (Do the opposite if you are left-handed.) You can then change grips as required, quickly and without effort. Tighten your grip only when you hit the ball.

Do not alter the angle of your hand or the natural spread of your fingers as you take hold of the racquet. *Cover as much of the grip as you can.* It gives you better control of the racquet.

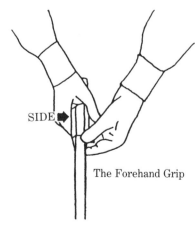

SIDE ▶

The Forehand Grip

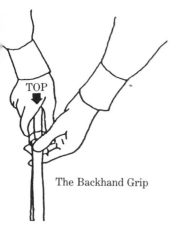

The Backhand Grip

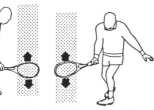

All Forehand and Backhand Shots the Same Vertical Plane

t 1 Straight Stroke

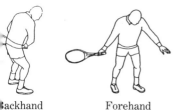

Backhand    Forehand

1   Loop Stroke

Backhand    Forehand

# Your Hitting Areas

You must know where your hitting areas are in order to time your strokes. A stroke cannot be timed unless you can measure the ball between two points: *from where it's hit to your hitting area.*

Find your hitting area for each stroke by swinging your racquet forward until it is in the same position as in the illustration.

Study the position of the racquet in relationship to your body. Note how far in front this is. *Visualize it. Remember it.* This is where you must try to take every ball. No matter *how high or low you take the ball, your hitting area is always on the same vertical plane.*

# How To Make a Forehand and Backhand Stroke

## LOOP STROKE VERSUS THE STRAIGHT STROKE

The difference between the loop stroke and straight stroke is that the straight stroke goes straight back and stops before swinging forward, whereas the loop stroke is a continuous, circular motion.

### Part 1: Straight Stroke

Pivot and turn sideways to the ball. Place the racquet straight back behind you at the natural length of your arm about halfway between your hip and knee. Keep your wrist solid.

### Part 1: Loop Stroke

Pivot and start your stroke up over your shoulder in a circular, looping motion.

**NOTE** *All movements of a loop stroke are the same as a straight stroke except that you are adding a circular movement to the stroke.*

Part 2   Straight Stroke and Loop Stroke

Backhand       Forehand

*Part 2: Straight Stroke And Loop Stroke*

Move into your hitting position. When the ball gets to your hitting zone, *drop the back part of your stroke below the ball* before you start your forward swing. Tighten your grip and hold your aimpoint as you hit. *Don't ever stop a stroke after hitting.* Let the racquet finish wherever its momentum takes it.

*Note the sameness in the strokes. The forward swing of the loop stroke and the straight stroke are the same.*

## PULL THE RACQUET

The forward swing of your forehand and backhand stroke should be started with *a slight pull from the heel of your hand. The pull is from the inside heel of your hand on the forehand and from the outside heel of your hand on the backhand.* Once you start your stroke, think only of where you want to hit. Hold a strong aimpoint, and your racquet will swing through the ball.

*The slight pull from the heel of your hand is essential to bringing the racquet into the ball correctly.* Most players are unaware of this technique. It's the primary reason for poor backhand strokes. *Pulling the butt of the racquet is the most important element in the development of a good backhand stroke.* Once you acquire the technique, your backhand troubles are over.

PULL          PULL

---

***Stroke tips***   Pivot your shoulders and *pull the racquet* to start your forward swing. Aim the ball and hold your aimpoint throughout the stroke.

---

# The Forehand and Backhand Topspin Strokes

Any stroke that starts under the ball and swings up and out imparts topspin. Use topspin strokes only on balls that bounce high enough for you to get your racquet under easily.

Make a Drop

*Part 1*

Drop the back part of your stroke down very low under the ball.

*Part 2*

Accelerate the speed of your racquet as it brushes up on the ball at the hit.

Accelerate Racquet Speed

The more you brush up on the ball, the more topsin manufactured and the more quickly the ball rises and falls. *To keep your racquet pressing out on the ball, be sure to hold a strong aimpoint* as you hit. Otherwise, your racquet will come off the ball too quickly, and the ball will be hit short, or into the net. The more spin, the shorter the shot.

The advantages of a topspin drive are:

• It delivers a powerful, high bouncing ball that's hard to handle.
• It's easier to keep in the court because the topspin pulls the ball down and reduces the risk of hitting it out of the court.

*Stroke tip*   *Don't try to use topspin on low balls.* You can't get your racquet far enough below a low ball to get a good hold of it, which increases your chances of making an error.

# The Forehand and Backhand Slice Strokes

The slice produces backspin, which provides more control but less power than flat or topspin strokes.

*Part 1*

To hit a slice, take the racquet back higher than the ball.

*Part 2*

Hold your aimpoint and use a slicing motion as you hit. Visualize how an axe cuts into a tree and you'll have a picture of what your stroke should be.

Use Slicing Motion

Allow your wrist to snap forward slightly as you hit. Experience will tell you how much to snap your wrist as your skill develops.

Hit with a *slightly* open racquet. Many players open the racquet too much. The more open the racquet face, the weaker the shots and the more mis-hits and floats.

 Closed     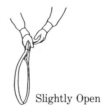 Slightly Open      Open

## USE OF THE SLICE

The slice is a good "change of pace" shot.
The slice provides more control against hard-hit balls.
The slice is a good stroke to use for certain approach shots down the line.

The slice can save points when you are out of position. It's a short stroke and can be prepared quickly. Sometimes just a snap of your wrist can help you make a shot that couldn't be made in any other way.

When you slice low balls, it produces a defensive shot with an upward trajectory that can be attacked. Aim the ball low over the net to make it less vulnerable.

## How To Make a High Forehand and High Backhand Stroke

SHORT BALLS THAT BOUNCE HIGHER THAN
THE NET

*Part 1: Forehand And Backhand High Drives*

Move alongside the ball with your racquet back and higher than the ball. *Start your forward swing with the heel of your hand.*

Heel of Hand

*Part 2*

Hold the racquet head up and do not let it drop as you meet the ball. Hit the upper part of the ball flat and hard. *Hold a strong aimpoint to force your stroke to swing out through the ball.*

Keep Racquet Head Up

# Solutions To Forehand and Backhand Problems Simplified

- **Wrong Grip**
- **Holding the Racquet too Tightly**
- **Winging on the Backswing**
- **Failing to Make a Drop on Low Balls**
- **Forward Swing Comes Down too Quickly**
- **Too Much Motion and Effort**
- **Poor Hitting Position**
- **Winging on the Forward Swing**
- **Breaking Your Wrist**
- **Failing to Pivot**
- **Swinging Across Your Body too Soon**
- **Failing to Hit Through the Ball**
- **Not Finishing the Stroke**

The following problems are the common causes of poor forehand and backhand strokes. Memorizing them will enable you to identify and correct the causes of most stroke problems and also prevent a lot of frustration.

**PROBLEM**   Wrong Grip

**SOLUTION**   Grips frequently slip. Check your grip and correct it between points. Pay attention to your grip until it becomes solid and natural.

If you're not changing your grip, it may be because you do not return your racquet to your other hand (the left in the case of a right-handed player) between shots or because you are holding the racquet too tightly. Be sure to *loosen your grip after hitting*.

A tight grip means:

**1.** You must open your hand in order to move it;
**2.** Then shift it to take the right grip;
**3.** And finally tighten it in order to swing.

That takes forever in relationship to a speeding ball compared with a loose hand that's free to move. Try it.

**PROBLEM**   Holding the racquet too tightly

Tightening your hand causes your forearm muscles to tighten and your arm to stiffen, destroying some of its capabilities.

**SOLUTION**   Hold the racquet gently. Hold your grip too loosely if necessary to keep your arm free. *Anything is better than tightening up*. Grip the racquet tightly *only* as you make contact with the ball. No one can hold a tight grip all the time without getting a sore arm.

Racquet Returned to *Other* Hand

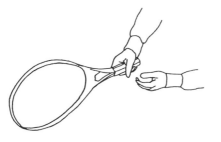

Winging on the Backswing

**PROBLEM**  Winging on the backswing

*"Winging" on the backswing is caused by trying to pre-pare your racquet without turning your body.* With your shoulder restricting the backswing, the only way you can get your racquet back is to "wing" out toward the sideline and then swing around your shoulder. That wasteful motion can cause errors against hard-hit balls because of the additional time it takes to prepare your racquet.

**SOLUTION**  Pivot your shoulder to allow your arm to swing back freely.

Pivot

Straight Back and Straight Forward

**PROBLEM**  Failing to make a drop on low balls

Failing to make a drop means cutting off the back part of the stroke and not getting your racquet below the ball before you hit. That causes the racquet to come forward on a downward trajectory and either drives a *low* ball into the net, or at the last moment slides underneath the ball and cups it, producing a float.

A Float

Into the Net

**SOLUTION**  To give yourself room to make a full drop, you must *keep the ball in front of you by visualizing your hitting zone and adjusting your feet.* If the ball gets in too close to you, your stroke will be cut off in order to hit.

*Loop Strokes: Making a drop* means dropping the racquet below the ball before you swing forward to hit. The *drop* is the back part of the loop stroke beginning at its highest point where the racquet begins to fall behind you to a point below the ball. A full drop adds power to your stroke and gets your racquet under the ball. *Accentuate* the drop: Reach back to complete the top part of the loop, then let the racquet fall and try to "feel" the drop.

Make a Drop

*Straight Strokes:* Take the racquet back at the natural length of your arm. The *drop* is simply a matter of placing your racquet below the ball.

Racquet Back Lower than the Ball

Keep Moving and Hold Aimpoint

**PROBLEM**   Forward swing comes down too quickly when hitting short, high bouncing balls

High forehand and backhand forward swings coming down at too sharp an angle cause the shot to go into the net. Not moving through the ball or not holding an aimpoint causes the swing to come down too quickly.

**SOLUTION**   Prepare the racquet higher than the ball. *Do not make a drop when hitting short, high bouncing balls.* Keep moving as you hit. Hit the upper part of the ball, and hold a strong aimpoint. That will compel you to swing out through the ball and your stroke to come down in a more gradual manner.

153

**PROBLEM**   Too much motion and effort

Using too much motion and effort will throw you off balance, create tightness, and prevent you from making a good stroke.

**SOLUTION**   Don't spread yourself out. Stay collected. Stay balanced and graceful as you swing. Measure the ball as it comes into your hitting area, and *be too slow rather than too quick to hit.* Keep yourself free of excessive motion. A good hit takes primarily timing and rhythm, not a lot of effort. Save your energy to work on the ball.

**PROBLEM**   Poor hitting position

**SOLUTION**   One of the main reasons for poor strokes is a *poor hitting position. Never take your eyes off the ball,* and measure your way to it. Use small steps as much as possible to get into a good hitting position. As you get ready to hit, *visualize two lines toward your aimpoint: one for the ball and one for your body alongside the ball.*

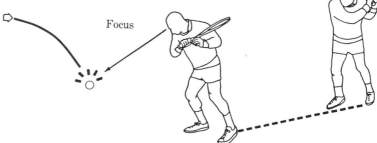

Focus

**PROBLEM**   Winging on the forward swing

"Winging" means *starting the racquet out toward the sideline* instead of straight into the ball. That is caused by not pivoting your body out of the way before you swing forward. Your racquet is forced to "wing" out in order to get around your body and into the ball.

Winging

**SOLUTION**   Pivot your shoulders to get your body out of the way and free your stroke to come straight into the ball.

On all your groundstrokes, *start the forward swing by pulling with the heel of your hand.* That pulling motion is so slight that it's almost more of a thought than a motion, but it's a vital part of your stroke because it helps bring the racquet straight forward into the ball correctly.

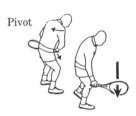

Pivot

Pivot

**PROBLEM**   Breaking your wrist

Using your knuckles to start the forward swing induces the wrist to break and *causes the racquet head to turn continuously* as it moves toward the ball. That makes timing terribly difficult because the racquet will be in the correct position to meet the ball for only a split second.

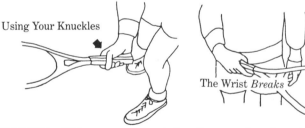

Using Your Knuckles

The Wrist *Breaks*

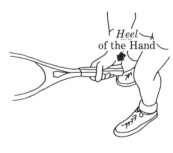

Heel
of the Hand

**SOLUTION**   When you start the forward swing into the ball, *pull and press out slightly with the heel of your hand.* That will help prevent your wrist from breaking and bring your racquet into a better position to meet the ball.

**PROBLEM**   Failing to pivot

One of the major causes of failing to pivot is not having your front foot planted when you hit. Therefore, you have no base on which to pivot.

155

**SOLUTION**   Turn sideways, *get your front foot down,* put your weight on it, and pivot your body into the shot.

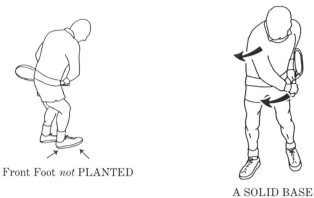

Front Foot *not* PLANTED

A SOLID BASE

**PROBLEM**   Swinging across your body too soon

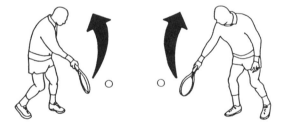

**SOLUTION**   Players who fail to hold an aimpoint make too many errors out the far sideline because their strokes come off the ball and cross their bodies too soon. *Hold your aimpoint,* and the racquet will go straight into the ball and stay on the line of the shot longer before swinging across your body.

**PROBLEM**   Failure to hit through the ball

This is caused by fear of missing and failure to hold an aimpoint.

**SOLUTION**   Hold your aimpoint and hit hard until you hit several balls in the court. *Don't be afraid to step in and hit. Be afraid not to.* Hitting through the ball is what holds the ball on the racquet by causing the strings to form a pocket and the ball to compress. Otherwise, the strings stay flatter and the ball flies off the racquet.

**PROBLEM**   Not finishing the stroke

*The stroke collapses at the same time that your mind drops the aimpoint.*

**SOLUTION**   Pick an aimpoint and hold it in your mind throughout the shot. Aimpoints are so essential that a review of Lesson 5 at this point would be wise.

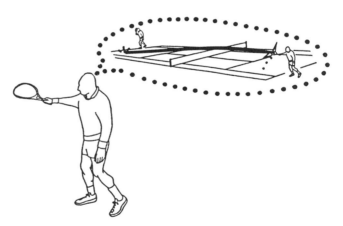

Hold Aimpoint as You Hit

# The Forehand and Backhand Volley Strokes Simplified

- **Volley Hitting Areas**
- **Volley Grips**
- **How To Make a Forehand and Backhand Volley Stroke**
- **The Forehand and Backhand Slice Volley**
- **Low Volleys**
- **High Volleys**
- **Wide Volleys**
- **Volley Footwork**
- **How To Make a Half Volley**

## Volley Hitting Areas

**REMINDER**   Your hitting areas are exactly the same for all strokes.

Swing your racquet and stop it at your hitting area. Your volley hitting areas are all on the same vertical plane.

Move your racquet up and down and study its position in relationship to your body. Note how far in front this is. Visualize it. Remember it. All your volleys should be taken on this vertical plane. Visualize your hitting areas in order to help time your volleys.

Hitting Areas are on Same Vertical Plane

## Volley Grips

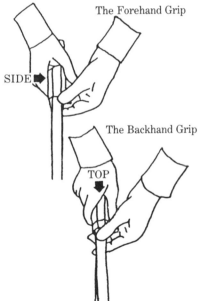

The Forehand Grip

SIDE ➡

The Backhand Grip

TOP

Use your regular forehand and backhand grips. It's easier to volley and easier on your arm. Some players prefer a continental grip because they don't have to change grips. Both styles are used by tournament players. The average players will do better using their regular forehand and backhand grips.

Some players claim that there isn't time to change grips. Not so. Players who have that problem are holding the racquet too tightly between volleys. Hold a relaxed grip between shots and you can switch grips easily.

## How To Make a Forehand and Backhand Volley Stroke

*Part 1*

Get in a "platform" position when your opponent is ready to hit. Stay bouncy on the balls of your feet. From that position you can judge the ball and get off to a quick start toward it.

Bouncy Platform Position

**REMINDER**   Many players make the platform too late. The ball jams them while they are still in the process of making it and there's no time to make a good stroke. It's better to make the platform a step too soon rather than a step too late.

Player Jammed;
Ball taken too Far Back

*Part 2*

*Visualize volleying the ball while it is coming in an up trajectory.* Try to hit every volley as the ball is coming up from as close to the net as you can get. These are the easiest volleys to attack and put away.

EASIER VOLLEY

TOUGH VOLLEY

*Part 3*

Move forward to volley the ball as close to the net as you can. As it reaches your hitting zone, pick an aim-point. Prepare your racquet by pivoting your shoulders and simultaneously snap your hand against your wrist. *Prepare your racquet higher than the ball.* The more you want to angle the ball, the higher it should be prepared.

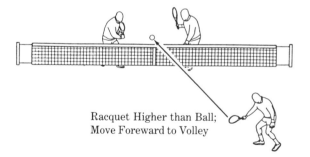

Racquet Higher than Ball;
Move Foreward to Volley

*Stroke tip*   *Looking at the top of the ball will help you get your racquet up higher than the ball.*

Hold your aimpoint. Start your stroke by pressing forward with the heel of your hand. Move in alongside the ball and hit.

**REMINDER** Don't think about hitting the ball. Think of *where* you want to hit and of moving *into* the ball. Don't worry. You'll hit the ball when it gets to your hitting area. *It's instinctive to hit or brush away an object coming at you. It's not instinctive to move into a projectile nor is it instinctive to aim it. Both of these skills are acquired talents. Both require deliberate thought until they are thoroughly programmed.*

Hold Your Aimpoint!

## The Forehand and Backhand Slice Volley

Slicing gives you more control, particularly when you're out of position. When you're in a jam, sometimes slicing with just a flick of your wrist can save a point. The slice is also an effective way of making angle volleys.

HOW TO MAKE A SLICE VOLLEY

*Part 1*

(Place the inside of your index finger on the beveled part of the racquet.) Take the racquet back higher than the ball. Keep your backswing short and in front of your shoulder.

*Part 2*

Take the ball in an up trajectory and aim. Use the heel of your hand to start your racquet forward, and hit through the upper outside part of the ball in a slicing motion (like chopping into a tree). Hold the aimpoint firmly in your mind until you've finished the stroke.

Take Ball in UP Trajectory—Aim and Slice

161

## How To Make a Low Volley

   Start your racquet higher than the ball. Get down as close to the height of the ball as you can by bending your knees. *Stay down* until you have finished the stroke. Keep your eyes on the ball. Aim low over the net and deep in the court.

   *Hit low volleys with tender loving care, or you'll hit them out.* The trajectory of the ball is up. Therefore, it won't take much to knock it out.

## How To Make a High Volley

   Special effort is required to volley balls that are above your head but not high enough to hit with an overhead. Trying to keep your eyes on the ball at this height is not easy. The back of your neck is somewhat strained and uncomfortable. Therefore, whenever you get a high ball like this, *be aware of the discomfort you are supposed to feel.* This will help you to keep your eyes on the ball and make the volley.

## Wide Volleys

When stretching wide, stay wide.

*When you are forced to stretch wide* in desperation to reach the ball, do *not* hit cross-court. Instead, *stay wide* with your racquet by aiming the ball *down the line*. The racquet will stay on the ball longer, and you'll have a better chance of making the shot.

It's hard to go cross-court while stretching wide because it's so tough to get far enough behind the ball to get good hold of it. The chances are the ball will slide off your racquet and you'll make an error.

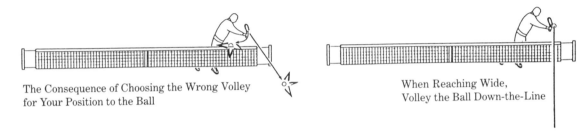

The Consequence of Choosing the Wrong Volley for Your Position to the Ball

When Reaching Wide, Volley the Ball Down-the-Line

## Volley Footwork

On volleys, your front foot should hit the ground *at the same time* that your racquet meets the ball. When your stroke starts above the ball and you step forward simultaneously, all your forces are moving down together imparting maximum power into the shot.

When your front foot gets down too soon, step forward with your other foot. Otherwise, your stroke will be restricted.

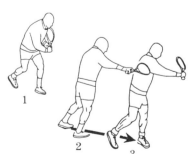

1
2
3

### CUT OFF THE ANGLE!

Don't move sideways. Visualize taking the ball as it's coming up and move diagonally to cut off the angle. *The sharper the angle of the shot, the straighter you must move in to intercept it.*

Cutting off the angle means:

**1.** The distance to the ball is shorter.
**2.** A chance to volley the ball earlier.
**3.** You're hitting from closer to the net and can make safer volleys.
**4.** More aimpoints to choose from.
**5.** Less time for your opponent to get to the ball and hit.

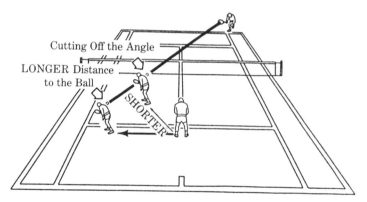

## How To Make a Half-Volley

Move into the ball. Use a short backswing and get down low to the ball by bending your knees. Aim the ball deep. Tighten your racquet grip. Hold your aimpoint and press your racquet firmly into the ball as it comes off the ground. Stay down low until you have finished the stroke.

# Solutions To Volley Stroke Problems Simplified

- **Racquet Lower Than the Ball**
- **Holding the Racquet too Close to Your Body**
- **Too Big a Backswing**
- **Gripping the Racquet too Tightly**
- **Failure to Snap Your Racquet Against Your Wrist**
- **Preparing Your Racquet Without a Pivot**
- **Breaking the Wrist**

**PROBLEM**   Racquet lower than the ball

When your racquet is prepared lower than the ball, there's no time to readjust and get it up higher than the ball, and then swing forward to volley. The result is that your racquet hits the side or under part of the ball, producing either an error or a weak volley.

Racquet Must Stop
at Top of Stroke

***Example***   When your racquet is prepared lower than the ball, you must lift it above the ball before you can volley correctly. This takes time. There's also a *time lag* at the top of your swing where the racquet must stop before you can swing it forward. Try it.

**SOLUTION**   Prepare your racquet up higher than the ball—*too high rather than too low* and your chances of making a good volley are much better. If your racquet is too high and you get a low ball, your hand can move down swiftly in one swooping motion with no hesitation or time lag, and you can still make the volley.

**PROBLEM**   Holding the racquet too close to your body

Holding the racquet in close causes it to go back too far behind you as you pivot to prepare it. That induces you to take the ball late, making it harder to judge and uncomfortable to hit.

**SOLUTION**   Hold the racquet several inches farther forward and away from your body than you ordinarily would in your ready position. Now when you pivot to prepare your racquet, it will be in front of you; the ball will be easier to judge and the volley easier to make.

**PROBLEM**  Too big a backswing

Don't use too big a backswing to prepare your volley stroke. When the ball comes quickly there isn't time to make a big backswing.

If you are in perfect position and the ball is coming slowly enough for you to judge easily, a big swing on the volley is OK. On most shots, however, you won't read and react to the ball quickly enough to get away with it. The timing is too critical.

**SOLUTION**  *Take a short backswing, aim, and hit through the ball.* Your volley will start to improve immediately.

**PROBLEM**  Gripping the racquet too tightly

Tightening your hand causes your forearm muscles to tighten and your arm to stiffen, destroying its mobility.

**SOLUTION**  Hold the racquet gently. Keep your grip loose if necessary to keep your arm free. *Anything is better than tightening up.* Grip the racquet tightly *only* as you make contact with the ball.

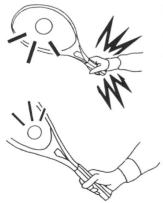

Hand Breaks from Pace of Ball

Racquet Snapped against Wrist;
Hand doesn't Break

**PROBLEM**  Failure to snap your racquet against your wrist

**SOLUTION**  Snap your racquet back against your wrist and the bone in your arm acts like a brace to support it. If you don't, your racquet is in a weaker hitting position. A ball carrying a lot of pace can cause your hand to break, especially if you take it late.

**PROBLEM**   Preparing your racquet without a pivot

Taking the racquet back with your hand instead of by pivoting means that your volleys will be less powerful. Without a pivot your body is open, and all you have to hit with is whatever power your arm can produce.

**SOLUTION**   The moment you read the ball, *pivot your shoulders to take the racquet back*. That also coils your body. Now as you pivot forward, you have all the power of your shoulders and your arm to release as you step in to volley. The pivot is particularly valuable when you're unable to step into the ball.

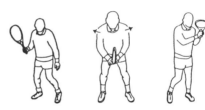

Using Your Knuckles

**PROBLEM**   Breaking the wrist

Breaking the wrist is caused by starting the forward swing with your fingers or knuckles. The result is that the racquet head is turning throughout the stroke so that it is in correct position to hit for a split second only. That makes it impossible to time the swing consistently and make solid contact.

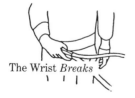

The Wrist *Breaks*

**SOLUTION**   Start your stroke forward by putting pressure in the heel of your hand, and think of pressing out on the ball. That will keep your wrist from breaking and your racquet solid at the hit.

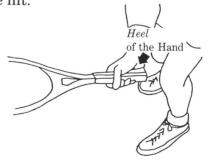

Heel of the Hand

# The Serve Simplified

- **The Service Grip**

- **Lining Up to Serve**

- **How to Serve**

- **Where to Aim Your Serve**

- **The Flat Serve**

- **The Slice Serve**

- **The Spin Serve**

- **The Toss**

- **Solutions to Tossing Problems**

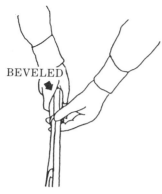

BEVELED

The Service and Overhead Grip

# The Service Grip*

Hold the throat of the racquet in your left hand. Place your index knuckle on the slanted (or beveled) part of the racquet handle (service and overhead grips are the same). Do not grip the racquet tightly. Keep your right arm straight from elbow to fingers. Do not allow your wrist to break.

Lining Up

# Lining Up To Serve

Stand sideways and spread your feet comfortably. With your feet spread, your legs act like a brace. Your body is now on a solid base, and you can shift your weight from one foot to the other without losing your balance.

When serving to the *deuce court,* line up behind the baseline just to the *right* of the center mark.† When serving to the ad court, line up behind the baseline about three feet to the left of the center mark.‡

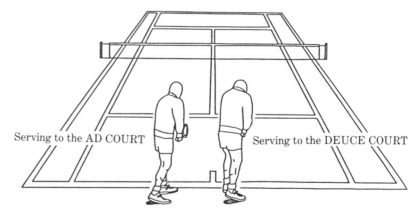

Serving to the AD COURT          Serving to the DEUCE COURT

*Service grips, like other grips, may vary. In the case of the service grip, however, be sure that it varies toward the backhand. Serving with a forehand grip does not create enough spin to keep the ball in the court consistently.

† For singles play. For more on this, see pp. 113–115.

‡ If left-handed, line up 3 ft to the right of the center mark when serving to the deuce court and next to the center mark if serving to the ad court.

# How To Serve

The power in your serve and overhead depends on the momentum of your racquet when it hits the ball. That momentum is generated by the use of your index knuckle. Your index knuckle should start your forward swing. Hold your aimpoint throughout the stroke, and the rest of your body will be pulled into the shot in a natural way. Learn to use your index knuckle handily and you'll develop a "clever" racquet. When all seems lost, a "clever" racquet can pull you out of many tight spots during a match.

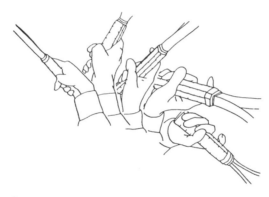

*Part 1*

Part 1

Line up with your weight on your forward foot and your racquet pointing at the court you're serving into. Hold the ball in the first three fingers of your tossing hand. Take hold of the racquet with your service grip and rest it on the fourth and fifth fingers of your tossing hand in a relaxed manner.

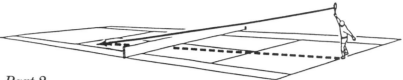

Part 2

Part 3

Part 4

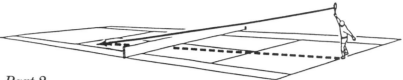

### Part 2

Select your aimpoint. Visualize a line along the ground from your front foot to your aimpoint. Raise this line in the air to your hitting area. Visualize it to your aimpoint. Don't use a lot of effort swinging your racquet back. Just let your racquet fall away from your ball hand as both hands drop simultaneously. Allow the racquet face to open as it falls. Your weight should shift to your back foot as your racquet goes back.

### Part 3

Lift both hands, extend your tossing arm completely before tossing the ball up to your hitting zone. As the racquet falls into place behind your back, get your elbow as high as you can. Getting your elbow up high will make it easier to get your racquet up over the ball and add power to your serve. Measure the ball as it reaches your hitting area.

### Part 4

Pivot and as you turn square to the net, visualize hitting over the very top of the ball (the part you can't see). Tighten your grip, hold your aimpoint, and use your index knuckle to roll your racquet forward over the top of it*—and step into the ball.

*When you look up at a ball, you see the under part or side of the ball and that's the part you tend to hit. By visualizing hitting the top of the ball, which you cannot see when it's up in your hitting area, it induces your swing to go up and hit higher over the ball.

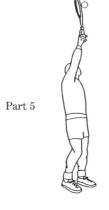

Part 5

*Part 5*

Hit the upper inside part of the ball.† Hold a strong aimpoint. That will compel you to press your racquet out on the line of the ball to your aimpoint.

Hold Strong Aimpoint

## Where To Aim Your Serve

Each service court contains four basic aimpoints:

**1.** Up along the sideline.
**2.** The outside corner.
**3.** Down the center.
**4.** The inside corner (the "T").

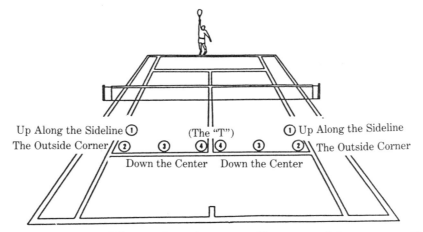

Up Along the Sideline ①    (The "T")    ① Up Along the Sideline

The Outside Corner ②   ③   ④④   ③   ② The Outside Corner

Down the Center    Down the Center

These aimpoints are all you need to serve well.

Keep it simple! Line up, visualize a line to your aim-point, raise the line in the air, toss the ball up on the line, and serve.

† For a flat serve.

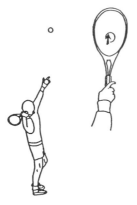

## The Flat Serve

The flat serve is called "flat" because hitting the upper center of the ball brings the racquet strings flat to the ball.

Try to hit the *upper inside part* of the ball. That induces more use of your index knuckle, which turns the racquet face inside out and brings it flat to the ball. Try it, it works!

The flat serve is the most aggressive serve and most powerful weapon in the game. It is also the most difficult serve to keep in the court because of the lack of spin and low trajectory over the net. The low trajectory of the ball makes it a poor serve for a short player to use.

Flat Serve to Inside Corner

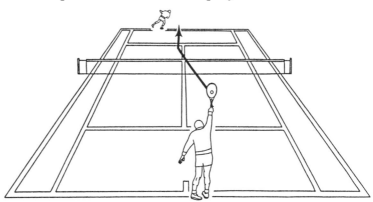

## The Slice Serve

To hit a slice serve, toss the ball to your right and closer to your head, and hit out over the *upper right-hand* side of the ball. Your arm will naturally tend to move up and across the ball, creating a higher trajectory and more spin.

The advantages of a slice serve are that:

**1.** The spin provides more control.
**2.** A well-developed slice serve hit to a sideline can have a vicious hook that takes the ball away from the receiver and out of the service court.

Toss Ball to the Right

**3.** It can be sliced into the body of the receiver.

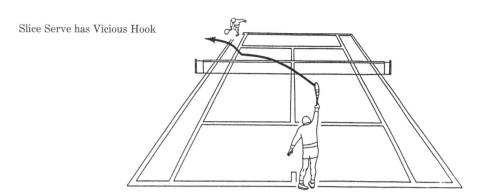

Slice Serve has Vicious Hook

## The Spin Serve

Hit Left to Right

To hit a spin serve, toss the ball directly over your head—or a little to the left—and hit up over the top of the ball *from lower left to upper right. Brushing up* on the ball sends it at a higher trajectory over the net, giving you a safer margin for error.

Hitting over the ball from left to right creates a big hop to the right.

The spin serve is especially effective as a second serve because it can be hit into the court more consistently than the other serves.

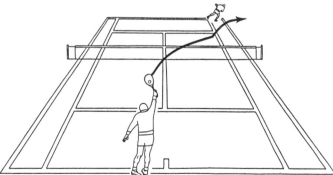

***Stroke tip*** The spin serve has less momentum than either the flat serve or the slice serve; so be sure to hold the thought of hitting out to minimize the loss of power.

## The Toss

The toss is a vital part of the serve. Players are often so concerned with hitting the serve that they pay too little attention to the toss. Nothing in tennis happens very much by accident, including placing the ball into the air correctly to serve. If you make a poor toss, catch it and start over.

### Your Tossing Area

Toss Ball to Your Hitting Area

Before you can toss the ball correctly, you have to know *where* to toss it. To find the correct spot in the air to toss the ball, put your racquet behind your back (see illustration), pivot, roll your hand forward until your racquet is vertical, and hold it there. Look at it. *Remember it!* Think of how far to the right and above your head it is. That is your hitting area. That's where you should toss the ball.

### The Toss for Baseline Play

Toss the ball so that the serve does not pull you too far past the baseline when you complete it. Every step you have to take to get back to your ready position behind the baseline makes it harder to get back in time to be ready for the service return.

### The Toss for Serve and Volley Play

Toss the ball as far in front of you as your serving capability will allow. The further in front you can toss the ball, the closer to the net you can get for your first volley.

### Tossing in the Sun

When you are facing the sun, you may not be able to see the ball if you toss it to your usual place. Try several test tosses to the right, left, or closer to your head until you find the spot where the sun is least bothersome. If you can't get away from the sun, line up a little to the right or left of where you usually stand.

## Solutions to Tossing Problems

**PROBLEM**   Not watching the toss

Players look up in the air as they start the toss and don't see the ball until it passes their line of vision. That time lag in seeing the ball gives them less time to judge the ball and can be the difference between making a good serve and a poor one.

**SOLUTION**   Focus your eyes on the ball from the beginning of your toss to the end of your serve.

Players generally toss the ball too quickly for their eyes to follow. Focusing on the ball in your tossing hand will force your toss to slow down and go up at a speed that your eyes can follow. Slowing your tossing arm will slow down your service motion, giving you better rhythm and more time to judge the ball before you serve.

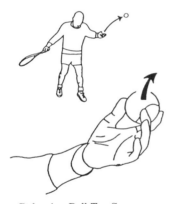

**PROBLEM**   Releasing the ball before your arm is fully extended (throwing the ball)

Releasing the ball too soon induces the elbow and sometimes the wrist to break. As a result, the ball is *thrown* up toward the hitting area instead of being *placed* there.

Releasing the ball before your arm is fully extended tends to make it roll off the tips of your fingers with forward spin, causing the toss to be low and too far ahead of you. Try it.

Throwing the ball creates other problems as well. First, it is an abrupt motion which disturbs the service rhythm. Second, the toss is difficult to judge because the ball rises too quickly for your eyes to follow. Third, it's more difficult to toss the ball consistently to the same spot.

Releasing Ball Too Soon

**SOLUTION**   Keep your arm straight and lift your hand gently as far as you can toward the exact spot in the air where you want to place the ball before releasing the toss. If you make a poor toss, catch the ball and start over.

Extend Hand Fully
Before Releasing Toss

**PROBLEM**   Flipping your wrist as the ball is released
Flipping your wrist when your arm is fully extended
tosses the ball behind your head.

Flipping Wrist

**SOLUTION**   To make an accurate toss, keep your arm
straight from hand to shoulder. Lift your arm until it is
fully extended toward your hitting area before you toss.
Do not allow your wrist to break.

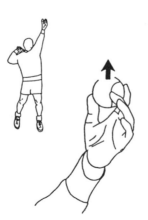

Keep Arm Straight Hand to Shoulder

# Solutions To Service Problems Simplified

- **No Aimpoint**
- **Lack Of Power**
- **Serves Hit Into The Net**
- **Serves Hit Beyond The Service Court**

Hold Your Aimpoint

**PROBLEM**  NO AIMPOINT

*No aimpoint means no accuracy.* Aiming for a general area instead of a specific spot will make your stroke indecisive and give you a bigger incidence of error.

**SOLUTION**  Line up with your racquet pointing to the court you're serving into. Choose a definite place in the court to aim to. Visualize a line from your front foot to your aimpoint and raise the line in the air to your hitting area. Hold this line firmly in your mind as you toss the ball up on the line, and hit out on the line to your aimpoint. Your hitting shoulder should be pulled out on the line and end up pointing directly to your aimpoint.

---

*Playing tip*  Remember that the actions of your body are created by your brain. The instant you let the aimpoint fade from your mind, your stroke will collapse. This is a major cause of poor serves. Players become so taken up with hitting the ball that they drop the aimpoint as they swing and wind up serving poorly.

Hold the line to your aimpoint firmly in your mind *all the way through the serve!* Once you know how to serve, then all you have to do is pick an aimpoint, toss, and serve to it.

---

**PROBLEM**  LACK OF POWER

The four most common problems that cause wasted effort and loss of power are:

**PROBLEM 1**  Servers grip the racquet too tightly on the backswing. This tightens the arm muscles and prevents the arm from swinging freely. A server with a constricted arm "muscles" the ball and cannot hit powerfully.

**SOLUTION**  Don't tighten your grip until you start the swing forward. Once your muscles are in motion, tightening your grip at the hit will not restrict their use, and you can hit with as much power as you want.

**PROBLEM 2**  Servers use themselves up by preparing their racquets with too much motion and effort. The result is tightness at the start of the forward swing, restricting the serve.

**SOLUTION**   Hold the racquet gently at the natural extension of your arms, which should be relaxed. When you start to serve, just let the racquet fall, lift your arm, and drop it behind your back easily. If you stay free and relaxed as you start the forward swing, you can use all your energy to generate power into the hit.

REMINDER: Don't use yourself up by making a lot of effort to get your racquet back. Stay loose and save your energy to work on the ball.

**PROBLEM 3**   Servers hurry their serve. Hurrying throws them off balance and disturbs their timing and rhythm. The result is tightness and inefficiency.

**SOLUTION**   You have complete control of the serve. There's no reason to hurry. Take your time to program yourself. Don't serve until you're comfortable, and don't rush your motions.

**PROBLEM 4**   Servers lose power if they strain to stretch upward beyond the normal range of their bodies. This causes them to tighten up, and then they can't use themselves efficiently to move forward and hit. Players strain upwards because they believe that they are increasing their power by doing it. Actually, when players go straight upward, their power *is wasted because it's going up instead of forward into the shot.*

**SOLUTION**   Don't *strain* upwards to hit. Your body should be *naturally extended* in order to generate maximum power. Always try to be in a comfortable position when you hit any ball. When you are strained beyond the normal extension of your body, your body is no longer collected, and you lose ease of motion and power.

STROKE TIP: HOW TO GENERATE POWER
To hit with power, visualize a line to your aimpoint, and maintain the rhythm of your stroke. Accelerate the velocity of your racquet by pivoting and using your in-

dex knuckle to speed the racquet head into the ball. Hit out straight on the line to your aimpoint. Now your racquet, arm, shoulder, hip, and foot will go forward on the *same* line bringing the additional momentum of your body into the shot.

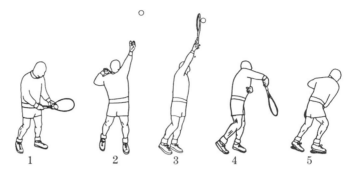

1    2    3    4    5

## PROBLEM    SERVES HIT INTO THE NET

A *low toss,* contrary to popular belief, is *not* the main reason for serving the ball into the net. If it were, kids would not be able to serve the ball. The primary cause is *failure to pivot your body out of the way completely before releasing the swing.* When you are lined up ready to serve, your body is blocking your forward swing. Without a complete pivot (turning your shoulders square to the net), your body remains in the way, preventing your stroke from extending fully forward through the hit. This forces your racquet to come down too soon and drives the ball into the net.

Try it. Stand sideways and try to swing without moving your left shoulder. You'll note that your body is blocking your swing and that the swing can't go out very far before it is forced down.

Swing Blocked

## SOLUTIONS    Three ways to correct hitting the serve into the net

1. Turn sideways and make a throwing motion. Keep your eyes on your left shoulder, and you'll see that your hand does not throw until your shoulder has pivoted out of the way. This is exactly what should happen when you serve. Many players are so eager to

Pivot

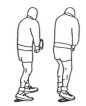

Player A     Player B

Right Foot Moved
2 or 3 inches toward
sideline

hit the ball that they release the swing before they complete the pivot and as a result hit the serve into the net. *Pivot your body out of the way of your swing.* Whenever you fault, think of the cause, in this case *not pivoting.* Before you serve again, make a shadow stroke and try to mentally feel yourself pivoting. On your next serve, concentrate on pivoting.

2. Use this solution on days when your timing and rhythm are completely off and you can't correct the pivot. *Move your back foot forward two or three inches toward the sideline.* This will partially pivot your shoulders and open your stance. A smaller pivot will help compensate for the lack of rhythm. Now you won't have as far to pivot to get your body out of the way of your swing.

**NOTE**   Player B has moved his right foot toward the sideline two or three inches. This has placed him in more of a semi-open position, requiring less of a pivot.

Try both stances!

3. *Toss the ball closer to your head or a little behind it.* This will cause your racquet to brush up on the ball more and hit it at a higher trajectory over the net.

**PROBLEM**   SERVES HIT BEYOND THE SERVICE COURT

The problem lies at the start of the forward swing. If you start the swing by *raising your arm and then snapping your racquet forward,* the racquet won't cover* (get over) the ball soon enough to keep it in the service court.

**SOLUTION**   When you decide to swing, roll your racquet forward immediately. Start the forward swing with your index knuckle to roll your racquet over the top of the ball.

*Definition of cover: As you roll your racquet into the ball, at one point your racquet is in this position over the ball (as shown in the illustration). I call this the "cover." If you start your swing by raising your arm first, the cover does not get over the ball soon enough to keep it in the service court.

183

# The Overhead Simplified

- **The Overhead Grip**
- **Your Hitting Area**
- **How To Hit An Overhead**
- **The Backhand Overhead**
- **Overhead Footwork**
- **Aiming The Overhead**

Many players are filled with trepidation at the thought of hitting overheads. The overhead is just another tennis shot and is really not very difficult.

Anybody can learn to hit overheads in good style in just a short time. Overheads are showy, fun shots that everybody loves to hit once they can do it.

## The Overhead Grip

*The overhead grip is the same as the service grip.*

BEVELED

The Service and Overhead Grip

## Your Hitting Area

To find your hitting area, place your racquet behind your back (see illustration), pivot, roll your hand forward from behind your back until your racquet is vertical. Hold it there. *Look at it.* Study its position. Think of how high it is above your head. *Visualize it!* Remember it! To time your stroke, it's essential to have a strong image of this area in your mind. This is where you should hit the ball. *It's the same hitting area as for your serve.*

The Overhead and Service
Hitting Areas are the Same

## How To Hit an Overhead

Elbow High
on Backswing

*Part 1*

As your opponent lobs the ball, lift your racquet straight back, turn sideways, and spread your feet so that you feel that you are on a solid base. Keep your hand and arm loose and relaxed. Get your elbow up high.

Use Index Knuckle
to Start Swing

## Part 2

Move to a comfortable hitting position. Select an aim-point and measure the ball as it falls into your hitting area. Start your pivot with your front shoulder. As you turn in to the ball, use your index knuckle to roll your racquet forward to hit.

Top

## Part 3

Tighten your grip, hold the aimpoint in your mind, hit the topmost part of the ball and step into it. (Think of serving the ball to your aimpoint. It's the same motion.) Your hitting shoulder should end up pointing toward the aimpoint.

Think of the Top of the Ball

# The Backhand Overhead

Backhand
Overhead
Grip

## THE BACKHAND OVERHEAD GRIP

Take a backhand grip, placing the thumb up the handle. This is best because you can use it effectively to roll your racquet forward.

*How To Hit A Backhand Overhead*

## Part 1

Place your racquet straight back over your backhand shoulder and raise your elbow high.

Elbow High

## Part 2

Move under the ball in the same way you would on your forehand overhead. Judge the ball. When it falls into your hitting area, pick an aimpoint, hold it in your mind, and hit out, rolling your racquet forward and *out* over the top of the ball.

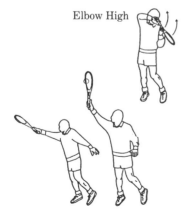

Roll Racquet up over
the Top of the Ball

186

Turn Sideways

## Overhead Footwork

Make a platform as your opponent is about to hit, and, as you read the ball, get your racquet back and turn sideways. From a sideways position it's much easier to walk, skip, or run. If your body is open, it's harder to get into a good hitting position. You could also lose your balance when you have to move backwards quickly.

*Don't hurry!* You can get to most overheads by turning sideways and walking or skipping to the ball in a collected manner.

Cross-Over Steps

If you can't get to the ball by skipping, then run back using cross-over steps and keep your eyes on the ball.

No matter what your footwork, your *last* step should always be *forward* on your hitting foot. Get your front foot *down* and hit.

If you're moving backwards and can't get your front foot down because the ball is getting past you, jump for the ball and throw yourself forward into it.

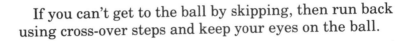

Jump and Throw
Yourself Forward

Roll Hand with
Maximum Speed

When the ball is behind you, you're in an unbalanced position when you hit. *The pressure of the ball and the lack of leverage in your arm can cause your stroke to stop as the racquet meets the ball and an error occurs.* The ball can be kept in the court by completing the stroke. To ensure it, put all your efforts into accelerating the speed of your racquet into the ball.

***Stroke tip***    If you let the aimpoint fade from your mind, the instant that you do, your stroke will collapse. This is a major cause of poor overheads. Don't become so anxious to hit the ball that you forget the aimpoint and miss the shot.

## Aiming the Overhead

Choose a definite place in the court to aim to, and remember your margin for error in from the lines. Visualize a line in the air from the ball to your aimpoint, and hit out on the line when the ball falls into your hitting area. Hold your aimpoint as you hit, and your hitting shoulder will be pulled out on the line and end up pointing directly to the spot you aimed to.

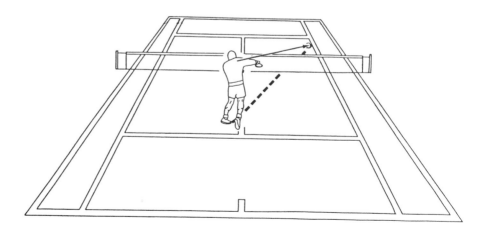

Aim the Ball

# Solutions To Overhead Problems Simplified

- **Lack Of Power**
- **No Aimpoint**
- **Poor Hitting Position**

**PROBLEM**  NO AIMPOINT

No aimpoint means no accuracy. Aiming for a general area instead of a specific spot will make your stroke indecisive and increase your incidence of error.

**SOLUTION**  Choose a definite place in the court to aim to and remember your margin for error in from the lines. Hold your aimpoint as you hit.

**PROBLEM**  POOR HITTING POSITION

A poor hitting position is caused by your anxiety to hit or by mis-judging the ball.

**SOLUTION**  Take your time. Keep judging the ball while you move into a comfortable hitting position. When the ball falls into your hitting area, measure, aim, and hit.

**PROBLEM**  MIS-HITS

Mis-hits are caused by poor timing or taking your eyes off the ball at the hit.

**SOLUTION**  Judge the ball and say "WAIT . . . NOW." As you hit, keep your eyes focused on the ball and your mind on your aimpoint.

**PROBLEM**  OVERHEADS HIT INTO THE NET

Overheads hit into the net are caused by dropping your aimpoint or failing to pivot your body out of the way of the stroke. Failing to pivot restricts the forward movement of your arm, which in turn causes your racquet to drop too soon and the shot goes into the net. If you are pivoting correctly and still hitting the net, it is because

you are failing to hold the aimpoint which causes your racquet to come down too soon.

**SOLUTION**   Pivot and hold the aimpoint as you hit.

**PROBLEM**   OVERHEADS HIT OUT OF THE COURT

1. The problem lies at the start of the forward swing. If you start the swing by raising your arm and then snapping your racquet forward, the racquet won't cover (get over) the ball soon enough to keep it in the court.
2. While you are waiting for a lob to drop to your hitting area, you are looking up at the bottom or the side of the ball. What you see many times is what you hit, and the result is that the ball goes out of the court.

**SOLUTIONS**

1. Project your mind to hitting the top of the ball. (The part you cannot see.) Hold this thought as you hit and use your index knuckle to snap your racquet forward into the ball. This will roll your racquet up over the upper part of the ball and keep your shot in the court.
2. If you do not get into a good hitting position and you must hit a ball that gets behind you, you must snap your racquet forward much more quickly to get the racquet over the ball than if the ball is in front of you. Otherwise, you'll hit the under part of the ball and hit the shot out of the court.

**PROBLEM**   LACK OF POWER

The four reasons that cause you to lose power on the overhead are the *same* as those that cause you to lose power on your serve.

---

*Stroke Tip*   HOW TO GENERATE POWER
   *You generate power on your overhead in the same way that you generate power on your serve.*

---

# Practice Simplified

- **The Importance Of Practicing**
- **How To Practice**
- **Ball Machines**
- **Backboards**
- **What Kind Of Matches To Play**

# The Importance of Practicing

The keys to good practice sessions are:

1. Always do what you are supposed to do with the ball, depending on your position to the ball and your position in the court.
2. Try to get into perfect position and try to make a perfect stroke every time.
3. Departmentalize your mind; think of only one part of the stroke at a time to perfect it.

While practicing any stroke, swing your arm free of your body. It should swing almost as a completely separate unit, so free it should feel like it doesn't belong to your body.

The importance of practicing *correctly* cannot be over emphasized. Practicing must be done with a definite plan to improve skills. Just hitting a lot of tennis balls without the right kind of thinking attached to it isn't going to do much for you. Practice the way you have to play.

No musician, for example, would practice just one note, at one speed, at one kind of pitch for very long. Musicians practice many different drills and rhythms as well as the same notes with varying degrees of aggressiveness in order to develop the touch required to make music. Tennis should be practiced in the same way.

While trying to develop a stroke be as slow and deliberate as possible. The slower you are, the more quickly you will learn because your brain has more time to understand what you are trying to do. Players miss the ball because they are too quick and eager to hit it.

Once your mind is programmed, you will produce whatever you are trying to do auto-visually. At this point, all you need to think about is aiming the ball.

When you make an error, think about the part of the stroke that broke up and caused the error. Reset the correction in your mind by slowly making a perfect practice stroke, feeling and visualizing the correct motion of the stroke to reset it in your mind. *Never end your practice on a bad shot. Always end your practice with a "good reflex" in your mind.*

*Measure Your Way To The Ball*

Pay more attention to getting into position to hit the ball than you do of your strokes.

As you perfect the use of your feet and get in better and better position to hit the ball, you'll find that your strokes will improve because you will be in a more comfortable position to use them. Tennis becomes largely a game of timing, movement, and aiming the ball when your strokes are developed.

## How To Practice

### USE A SYSTEMATIC METHOD

Use a systematic method in developing your game. Write down a monthly schedule of what you plan to practice, allocate the time for practice, and stick to it.

### SCHEDULING

Line up as many matches and practice sessions as far in advance as you can. This will save lots of time.

### NUMBER OF THINGS TO PRACTICE EACH DAY

Don't set up too many varied things to practice each day and don't change anything you're practicing until you become good at it.

### PARTNERS

The best way to practice is with a good partner and to plan before going out on the court exactly what you want to practice and the amount of time you intend to practice it.

*How To Practice Various Strokes*

### THE SERVE

Warm up thoroughly before you begin to practice serving. Don't practice your serve for more than fifteen or twenty minutes. Longer practice sessions may injure your

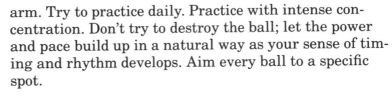

arm. Try to practice daily. Practice with intense concentration. Don't try to destroy the ball; let the power and pace build up in a natural way as your sense of timing and rhythm develops. Aim every ball to a specific spot.

## OVERHEAD

Be slow and rhythmic and don't use a lot of effort. Don't try to blast every ball. Take your time. As soon as the ball goes up, take your racquet back, turn sideways, get up on your toes, and think only of getting in position to hit. The last thing to think about is hitting the ball. Build a groove of aiming all balls at as big an angle as your position in the court will permit.

## GROUNDSTROKES

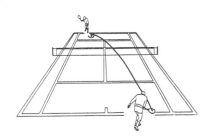

When practicing with a partner, don't stand too close to the sidelines.
EXAMPLE: If practicing cross-courts, stand behind the baseline about halfway to the sideline to allow space in the corner for your partner to hit to. If you both stand near the sideline, there's no room to hit the ball in the court.

## LOBS

Practice hitting lobs high and deep down the center from every place in the court. Practice running down balls hit over your head and lobbing them back.

## VOLLEYS

Stand in your ready position at the net. Stay on the balls of your feet and stay bouncy. When your body is mobile, it's easier to get to the ball. Start with volleying balls higher than the net, then lower, then varied. Start the racquet higher than the ball, aim the ball, take it as it's coming up, and walk into the ball as you hit.

Aim all volleys cross-court to start your practice. This will help you to take the ball more in front of you. Try to hit all high volleys at a sharp angle.

As your volley improves, start from a position further back from the net until you are starting from a point halfway between the service line and the baseline. Always move in on every ball until you are up to the net, then start the drill over again.

## Ball machines

Ball machines are wonderful to practice with if used properly.

1. Use good tennis balls.
2. Don't stand in one spot to hit balls coming out of the machine. The best way to practice is to move to the ball and hit.
3. For groundstrokes, stand at the center mark and place the machine so that balls are delivered to any area where you have to move to them.
4. Your purpose should be to see how perfectly you can get in position, aim, and make a perfect stroke.
5. Play the ball like a point. If you don't get there in good position to make the stroke you're practicing, throw the ball back. Aim every ball to a specific place in the court.
6. Practice lobbing from all parts of the court.
7. Set up the machine for high volleys, low volleys, short balls, high bouncing balls, and overheads. Always *move* to the ball, don't stand still, bounce lightly on the balls of your feet between shots. Work. Make the practice count.

## Backboards

Walls are best used by pupils who have developed the ability to hit the ball consistently in the court. The ball comes back too fast for beginners. Backboards are invaluable for grooving your strokes and improving your footwork.

Don't try to hit the ball hard. Keep it in play. Always aim the ball. If you have a wall where you can mark out some targets with masking tape, it will help your aiming considerably.

If the ball is getting back too rapidly for you to handle, stand further back and allow the ball to bounce twice until you can handle it. Practice one stroke at a time until you can return the ball in style, consistently. Next, alternate forehands and backhands. Next, hit wider and wider, forcing yourself to run for the ball. Swing all the way through the ball; never stop a stroke. Step in as you hit.

## What Kind of Matches To Play

When lining up your matches, don't try to play only better players. Ideally, you should play people at a level below you so you can practice whatever you choose and still win because there's not much pressure. Arrange matches with players at your own level. Here, there is maximum pressure because your level of play is the same, and a few careless errors by either of you could lose the match. Play matches with people a level or so above you, so that you are forced to try to raise your game to win.

Don't play matches with players too far above you. If you do, you won't get a chance to play much tennis because you won't get a chance to hit many balls.

*The World of Tennis*

One of the biggest advantages of playing tennis in today's busy world is that it doesn't require a lot of time to play. An hour or two will give most of you all the tennis you want at one time.

Tennis adds another big plus in its contribution to your health and sense of well being. Participating in a vigorous sport does much to keep you active and physically fit.

Despite the glamour at the top and the wishful thinking about how wonderful it would be to be up there, the players who probably have the best of the tennis world are those who play tennis throughout their lives.

Life from time to time becomes a humdrum affair, and during these periods the need for something personal to do becomes urgent and necessary to our happiness. Tennis is a lifetime sport that can take up this slack in life.

By its nature, tennis is a personal achievement sport, and as such, belongs to each player in a very private and special way. Tennis is completely individualistic. What you do with it is yours alone.

Goals in tennis are virtually unlimited. The opportunity is always there if you wish to find out how far you can go in the game. There are local, regional and national tournaments for every age group scheduled throughout the year. No matter what your age, you can always improve.

Life is suddenly more satisfying if the gaps of monotony in our lives are filled by an activity that provides a sense of achievement and joy.

Tennis does it all!

# Index